The Literature of Cinema

ADVISORY EDITOR: **MARTIN S. DWORKIN**
INSTITUTE OF PHILOSOPHY AND POLITICS OF EDUCATION
TEACHER'S COLLEGE, COLUMBIA UNIVERSITY

THE LITERATURE OF CINEMA presents a comprehensive selection from the multitude of writings about cinema, rediscovering materials on its origins, history, theoretical principles and techniques, aesthetics, economics, and effects on societies and individuals. Included are works of inherent, lasting merit and others of primarily historical significance. These provide essential resources for serious study and critical enjoyment of the "magic shadows" that became one of the decisive cultural forces of modern times.

Opportunities

in the

Motion Picture Industry

Photoplay Research Society

ARNO PRESS & THE NEW YORK TIMES

New York • 1970

Reprint Edition 1970 by Arno Press Inc.
Reprinted from a copy in The Museum of Modern Art Library
Library of Congress Catalog Card Number: 73-124033
ISBN 0-405-01633-6
ISBN for complete set: 0-405-01600-X
Manufactured in the United States of America

Opportunities
in the
Motion Picture Industry

—and how to qualify
for positions in its
many branches

Photoplay Research Society
Bureau of Vocational Guidance
Los Angeles, Cal.

Acting for the Screen

The Woman Making Up for the Screen

The Man Making Up for the Screen

Directing the Pictures

The Assistant Director

The Cameraman

"Still" Pictures

The Art Director

Art Titles

The Motion Picture Laboratory

The Film Editor

Designing Clothes for the Movie Folk

The Property Man

The Location Man

Operating a Projection Machine

The Exhibitor's Opportunity

Distributing Pictures on the State Rights Basis

Scope and Outlook of Visual Education

A Motion Picture Dictionary

Directory of Leading Motion Picture Studios

ACTING FOR THE SCREEN: THE SIX GREAT ESSENTIALS

By MARSHALL NEILAN

Editor's Note: There is probably no one affiliated wtih the motion picture industry better qualified to write on the subject of acting for the screen than Marshall Neilan. He has held every important post in a motion picture studio and knows the art from every possible angle. His rise to true motion picture heights crowns a career in the industry that has back of it a brilliant record of achievement.

WHEN an actor has gained distinction as a great comedian, he invariably expresses a desire to play Hamlet. When an actress has become famous for her ability to wring tears out of a stony-hearted skeptic, she is usually quoted as saying that she longs to play comedy. Some comedians have transferred their efforts to tragedy and with startling success. Some sob-sisters have gratified their ambition to play comedy, and have played it well. But these were the exceptions, and except in one or two cases, they have gone back to their original types.

There are, of course, some actors and actresses so versatile that they can enact any type of role, but most of them specialize in some particular sort of characterization. And why not? All other art forms are expressed in a variety of ways; one artist specializes in etchings, another uses pastels and a third will devote his time to portraits in oils. Each has, of course, mastered the technique and he could work with other media, but he is at his best when using that one with which he has specialized.

So it is with acting, and particularly acting for the screen. It is needless to mention the fact that the screen demands a great deal more from its recruits than does the stage. But this bugaboo has been greatly exaggerated, and has discouraged many persons who possess real talent.

The amateur, and particularly the woman, does not often realize the extent of her ability. The urge for expression is there, and the desire to act. Often her greatest asset lies in some little peculiarity that she has constantly bewailed.

In fact most of the "ifs" and "buts" that keep the average amateur from making her first try for fame in moving pictures result from the work of those pestiferous little devils, Super-Modesty and Self-Criticism.

For instance, says one pretty girl as she holds up the mirror to nature, "Oh, dear! Why did God get tired out when he started making my nose? Who can tell? I might have been a motion picture star but for that."

Says another dainty maid, taking a disappointed inventory of her personal charms, "I'm so thin, I'm afraid the camera would miss me, if I ever did get a chance to try for the movies."

Wails a third, "What good does it do me if my features are perfect as long as I haven't any personality?"

But you're all wrong, girls. You forget that the precious spark of fame and fortune comes many a time from just such a little personal eccentricity as yours. While you are not the type, perhaps, that you admire, so you fail to sell whatever marketable attributes you have *just* because you haven't Mary Pickford's eyes, or a smile like Constance Talmadge's, or the dash of Nazimova.

You must stop to think of one very important fact. *No one,* not even the starriest of these famous ones *has everything!* Some have more personal advantages than others. Oh, yes! We'll all agree on that. But just glance over the foremost constellation and see what you'll see. Everyone in the group has, perhaps, several points of attractiveness but you will note that in each case, one of the *six great essentials* to success has been featured to a more striking degrees than any of the others.

Sometimes this is true to such an extent that in your intense admiration, you are conscious of nothing less than perfection. *Yet,* with all due credit to these splendid artists who give us something to think about and dream about in our pleasure-seeking moments, perhaps if you could have a confidential boudoir chat with each one, she would tell you, with a bit of suppressed longing, of some little thing she wishes nature would do, or some little thing she wishes nature hadn't done for her. And you will be surprised to think you had never noticed the triviality of which she speaks, just because no one is, really, so mercilessly critical of us as we, ourselves, are.

But you are getting impatient to learn what are the *six great essentials*. And you shall have them. First of all, you know I'm going to say *beauty*. That, of course, needs no explanatory remarks. Another one is *personality*. Another, *charm* (there's a difference between these two that you'll understand later). Next there is *temperament*, then *style*, and sixth, *the ability to wear clothes*.

The most striking, and perhaps the most interesting way to force this truth upon your minds, is to point to six great favorites who have not only made a sensational hit but who have by subsequent achievements proved that their popularity is not a thing of the moment, but is based upon qualities and characteristics that are sure to attract today or a hundred years from today. There are many that we could choose as graceful embodiments of one or more of the *six essentials*, but after conscientious, impartial consideration of the screen's great galaxy of artists, we have selected what are perhaps the most striking examples.

For sheer *beauty*, perfection of features and a portrait-like magnificence, who can call forth more admiration than Katherine MacDonald? If you are attracted to her, you will instantly recognize that it is primarily her rare physical loveliness which appeals. The role makes very little difference with Katherine MacDonald. So long as she stays young and beautiful, we will continue to be awed worshipers at her shrine.

Hardly have we written the next essential, *personality*, when the magnetic name and presence of Mary Pickford flashes before you. You just need to recall one of her radiant smiles, one of her delightful impersonations, or one of her raggedy roles in which her natural personal charm was almost obscured in the intensity of her characterization, to realize that you love Mary Pickford, first, last and always, because she is Mary Pickford. She has something that irrespective of looks or age or anything else, will live on. She has *personality*.

Charm is a more quiet, a more subtle expression than is personality. It is none-the-less attractive, however, to many fans, as witness one of the most popular of its possessors, Elsie Ferguson. Something more spiritual, more elusive than personality, something that is enhanced by beauty but not necessarily dependent upon it, clings to this lady who has fittingly been called the aristocrat of the screen.

You are probably thinking that Norma Talmadge should have been included long before now, but an analysis of this attractive star's success places her in the forefront of those who hold their admirers through *temperament*. Often it is attributed to actresses but seldom possessed to such an extent as Norma Talmadge possesses it. It is her extreme sensitiveness to every possible emotion, her poignant response to a hundred different moods, which, expressed in vivid play of features and gestures, mark her as a truly superior personality.

Style, a semi-mental, semi-physical quality, is more superficial than the above characteristics. It depends not merely upon clothes, but upon an innate knowledge of how to walk, how to stand, how to conduct oneself generally. A number of comediennes can boast of it, but none more rightfully than Bebe Daniels. A poise that never flags, self-assurance, an accurate understanding of her best features, and the knowledge of how to "put herself over," are evident in everyone of this clever young woman's efforts.

The ability to wear clothes is no small asset. Is there anyone who can flaunt a superb wardrobe with more dash than Gloria Swanson? To the smallest detail of ornament such as a buckle on a headdress or a wrist trinket, this young woman has a knack of lending to her apparel a certain significance of modernity that makes you unconsciously think that whatever she happens to put on is, of course, *the very latest thing.*

The important question, is, which one of the *essentials* is yours? Most everyone of you has at least one of these. *First* of all, you must realize which is yours (that is not such a small task either, as self-knowledge comes with development, not nature). *Then,* you must cultivate this, emphasize

Lucille Ricksen and Her Dollies

Screen Children
Studying at Brunton Studios, Hollywood

Robert DeVilbiss
In "The Old Nest"

Lucille, Marshall and Mrs. Ricksen

Marie Morehouse
15 Months Old

it and perfect it until everyone about you is forced to recognize that you are beautiful, charming or chic, or that you have personality, temperament or style. The chances, ten to one, are that you have not merely one, but, as each of our six fair examples, several of these *essentials*. But there is *one* in which you excel. Which one is it? Study your mirror with a candid eye, and be sure, be very sure, that you are not too modest.

That is different advice, is it not, from what our grandmothers and Sunday School teachers give us? But the movie profession *is* different. It has brought forth new standards of self-appraisal. It requires a supreme confidence in all the gifts that the good Lord has bestowed upon us—mind you, not exaggerated idea of our own beauty or cleverness—but a strictly fair opinion, unhampered by supermodesty.

Your own personal experience reminds you that there are hundreds of beautiful girls, charming girls—hundreds of the other four kinds of girls—who will never get any closer to the screen than the front row of their favorite theatre. Perhaps the hosiery clerk in the biggest department store in your town has a face and figure more beautiful than has ever been photographed. That girl, if she only knew it, might be making $5,000.00 per week instead of eighteen.

You may not be quite as beautiful as she, *but*—you may have ten times her personality and brains.

Did you ever think of that? If not, think of it now and keep thinking of it. Don't listen to discouragement from "friends." Don't believe that there is some mysterious key to success in this particular profession. Don't believe that the gates are closed except to a few fortunate ones who know somebody who is assistant to some Great Person who holds jurisdiction over this profession.

Speaking as a director, I can give you a bit of interesting information. There is no such thing, among men of our profession, as being satiated with beauty or talent. We are none of us at the stage, professionally speaking, where we do not get a thrill from the first sight of anyone who has something new or distinctly pleasing to offer. There is no one of us who does not instinctively feel the urge to create something artistic when he sees a promising subject. Instantly there is the double-sided curiosity within us—first, "What am I capable of doing with this personality?" And second, "What can she do with herself?" From then on the work is co-operative—and fascinating.

Another very important consideration—

It may be that you are unusual enough, either in appearance or personality, to play, not a conventional leading role, but a strong character part. You may not have the qualifications of a screen idol, but you may be a type so true to life that you are indispensable to the screen. I have in mind a woman who, without youth or what is commonly known as beauty, and with no reputation whatever, startled the whole country with her marvelous characterization of a mother role. You will all remember Vera Gordon in "Humoresque." You will never forget her, will you? Because she fitted the conception of what a mother should be, and for no other reason whatever, she was assigned that role. As a result she has identified herself with this type of role, so that today, you can't think of Vera Gordon without thinking of a plump, wholesome, kind woman, who loves her children.

Less and less, as time goes on, does success in the movies depend upon mere prettiness. What you do with whatever ability you have counts far more. As in a sales office, so in a motion picture studio. Can you take orders? Are you receptive to honest suggestions from someone who has had the advantage of a wider experience than yours? If so, you have a great fundamental quality without which nothing can be accomplished.

Stars, as you may know, are never made overnight. Most of them "arrive" after months, maybe years, of hard labor—not work, but *labor,* spent in playing obscure parts. But if you have real dramatic talent, obscurity and competition cannot hold you down. You will in time force the director, your rivals, and the public, to admit that you are no longer an extra, or a secondary, or somebody's leading woman, but a star.

The field is a wide one. Never before has so alluring a profession held out a greater variety of opportunities to a greater variety of aspirants. The fruit crop is bounteous this year. Success is on every bough. Reach for it.

Let the pretty girl whom we referred to in the second paragraph take another, more tolerant view of her looks. She doesn't like her nose, she says, "It's too stubby." Now right there is where we differ with her. It may be stubby, but it isn't too stubby. Let her ask her boy friends who have been her admirers since the days of aprons and pigtails, or her new, grown-up beaus, what it is that they love about her. As sure as she wants to be a movie star, they'll say, "I don't know, sweetheart, unless its because you have such an adorable little nose!"

And the girl who never can grow fat, no matter how much buttermilk she drinks—let her stop and think a minute next time she sighs before a full-length mirror. Let her forget the plump beauty of her chum who patronizes her because she weighs only 98 pounds. Consider some of our slender screen fairies, who, far from disguising their slightness, deliberately accentuate it. You know them—Anita Stewart, Constance Talmadge, Lillian Gish, Nazimova. For that matter, any fashion magazine has pages and pages of encouragement for the girl who is not only slender but (oh! direful word) skinny. She can wear a style of clothes that is forbidden to any one with any inclination whatever toward stoutness.

The third little girl who bewailed her lack of personality has a snap, because as we said, she has the face of an angel. She can cultivate personality by cultivating an interest in persons and things outside her own immediate circle. She can test out her own conversational ability because people will always listen to her. She is so beautiful. The trouble with marvelously pretty girls is often that they are lazy, too lazy to be interesting. But with a little initiative and an incentive, they can develop that absurd, charming, magical something that we call *personality*.

In repetition, as the rhetoricians say, lies emphasis. In repetition also, we might add, lies monotony. We don't want to bore you but we do want to impress you with the great and mighty rule for success in the world of shadow-shapes. Don't underestimate your own distinctive charm, and don't, don't, don't indulge in a friendly folly of imitating when you can CREATE.

THE WOMAN MAKING UP FOR THE SCREEN

By MARY ALDEN

Creator of the Mother in "The Old Nest"

Editor's Note: To Mary Alden has fallen the happy lot of becoming the greatest exponent of make-up the screen has known. Her characterizations have all been masterpieces, and her work as the "mother" in "The Old Nest" stamped her as one of the screen's greatest emotional actresses. I feel happy, indeed, to be able to offer for your perusal this chapter. To those patrons of the silent drama interested in screen make-up, it will make fascinating reading—to all patrons of the silent drama it should make highly interesting reading.

GIRLS who have written to me, asking me to help them get engagements in motion pictures, have always assumed that youth and beauty and my assistance were all that was necessary to establish them as motion picture actresses. Not one has mentioned any special qualification other than beauty. Without any preparation or study they just decide to be motion picture actresses. Now, would they expect to earn a salary in any other profession without special preparation, just because they were beautiful? Youth and beauty are great assets, of course, but they will not carry one far in motion pictures unless they are combined with a developed artistic intelligence, capacity for hard work, and a spark of dramatic genius.

Beautiful moving figures are not dramatically interesting in themselves. To make the moving figure or character interesting the young beauty must be able to project some of the spirit that animates the soul of the character she is playing. This can only be accomplished through constant study of human nature, the habits, the thought processes, the ambitions and feelings of men and women, with all the external evidence left on the face, on the form and in the movement of the body.

To the young artist with the instinctive desire to express the beauty and truth about life who would choose the screen as a medium, I say study, study, study. Study every face, every woman that you meet. Try to put yourself in her place. See, hear, think with her. Make a persistent effort to understand human nature—life as it is, not as you would like to have it—but as it is. If you are earnest in your search for understanding you will find your bootblack as interesting as your favorite matinee idol.

What you most admire in the work of Miss Pickford or Miss Pauline Frederick is the result of months of nerve-racking labor in every play, years of study and experience plus a brilliant spark of genius. There are no short cuts to success in the art of acting, or in any other art.

Under the head of preparedness I should also advise a system of daily exercise to preserve the good health and to keep the body flexible and in tune. The body is the instrument through which you are going to reflect the music of your soul in emotion and movement, and it must be in tune to respond to your thought. The silent drama is not pantomime; dramatic action takes place in the mind, and physical movement is the motor counterpart to the mental drama. So it is most necessary to keep the body in a condition of quick response.

A close study of Mr. Chaplin's splendid art will help you to understand action more surely than I can explain it here. A body that is sagged and out of plumb is not going to carry a beautiful face very far. You can always get the effect of the sagged body with clothes, if the part calls for it, but you can only acquire a healthy, beautiful, responsive body through hard work and exercise.

I never realized how little I knew about the technique of make-up until I tried to explain the process. In creating a character, grease-paint is the last thing I think about.

After a careful study of the natural propensities, racial characteristics, affections, virtues, habits of thought and especially the frailties of the character that I wish to depict, the face, physical angles of form, and the tell-tale movement of the hands just compose themselves in my mind, like mental pictures of our favorite heroes, that we know so much about but have never seen. This study and analysis is most important, not only as a guide to make-up, but for the understanding of the character and the emotion and feeling produced in that character by the pleasant and unpleasant situations in which the author places it.

No two characters are alike, so there can be no set rules for make-up. One has to be guided entirely by this study, by imagination, observation and the suggestions of the author. Just as external influences produce different emotions in men and women, so these emotions produce different marked evidence on the features or form. Each character being differently constituted, it is differently affected by like influences, and the evidence marked out in grease-paint and line will be different in each case.

Of course, human nature and passions are the same the world over—they antedate civilization and intellectual culture, but habits, manners and thought processes differ greatly, so that what we discover about one characteh in the matter of make-up will have little application in the make-up of another character.

Mrs. Hutch in "Old Hutch," Helen Whipple in "The Witching Hour," Mrs. Rhead in "Milestones," and Mrs. Anthon in "The Old Nest," were as different in temperament, habit and feeling as "Mrs. O'Grady" and "The Colonel's Lady," although they were all just women under the skin. The make-up for each of these characters was as different as I could make it with grease-paint.

For illustration, we will take the eyes and brow of Mrs. Anthon and Mrs. Rhead—after forty years had marked them and life had scribbled little wrinkles around the eyes and above them. If wrinkles were the result of age entirely, I might have designed the same set of wrinkles for both characters, but wrinkles are really the result of thought processes upon certain groups of muscles, which pucker and contract under the influence of emotion. Mrs. Anthon of Carthage, U. S. A., the unselfish, sympathetic little mother of six children, domestic in her habits, with a highly developed maternal instinct, had not the keen sense of humor that forever sparkled in the bright eyes of the selfishly happy little Mrs. Rhead, the spoiled wife of a rich builder of Kensington, Gore, England.

Mrs. Rhead, with her mid-Victorian manners and ideals, was lacking in maternal instinct. Selfishly in love with her husband, she was neither touched nor influenced by anything but her husband, John Rhead, and his opinions. Consequently, those little lines that revealed this difference in character, took a difference in position and direction in each case. The soft, sympathetic eyes of Mrs. Anthon were dulled with grief at forty, after the death of her eldest son. Anxiety about the future of her other children, and dejection after they left home, exercised the corrugator muscles at the inner end of the eyebrow with deep lines above, in the forehead. As time went on and her loneliness grew almost unbearable, habitual contraction of these muscles developed little ridges at the inner end of the eyebrow, with little vertical furrows between them, just above the bridge of the nose. The contraction of the upper orbicular muscles around the eyes, in weeping, hollowed out deep depressions over and under the eyes. All the sweet gentleness of her nature was revealed in the soft, sad expression of these eyes.

Now, because happiness and the habit of smiling exercise and develop other groups of muscles, Mrs. Rhead's brow and eyes were differently marked. Habitual happiness draws the muscles of the face up and back, and as happy people usually have better health and blood circulation, we find lines more lightly traced, except those left by the muscles that come into play in smiling and laughing.

The long, horizontal lines on Mrs. Rhead's brow were lightly marked, the eyebrow stretched nearly straight and slightly high. The keen sense of humor and ready smile, that took the sting out of her selfishness, contracted the lower orbicular muscles, drawing up and back the muscles at the outer corner of the eyes, known as laughing wrinkles. Mrs. Rhead's eyes always sparkled with quick change of expression. Her selfishness was revealed in the shape and movement of her mouth, just as Mrs. Anthon's mouth revealed her deep sympathy and lack of humor.

In motion pictures we are limited in the use of color to those colors that photograph black or white. As the tone of the skin changes with age and exposure, different shades of grease-paint are employed to blot the age and texture of one's own skin, and as far as possible, all the character that is revealed in mouth and eyes. With the

Mary Alden

mental picture developed through the study of character as my guide, I experiment for days with different tones and colors, trying to mould my own face into one that will resemble the picture in my mind. Photographic tests are taken of each effort and it is then that we discover that what convinces the eye will be lost on the lens of the camera.

I usually complete my make-up looking like a design in Batik, because I get my best results with the use of purple, blue, brown and red, for lines and moulding.

Careful arrangement of the hair will make the face appear long or round. It is not easy for a woman to push back the hair line without shaving the hair, but it can be easily lowered by small, carefully fitted pieces of false hair.

In making up as the mulatto in "The Birth of a Nation" I lowered the hair line an inch and a half by the use of a false piece pasted across my forehead. Small appliances of my own manufacture, placed inside the nostrils, hurt dreadfully, but gave me the flat broad nose not unlike that of the mulatto girl that I had engaged—ostensibly as a maid, but really as a study. A layer of cotton under the upper and lower lips, and careful drawing with lip rouge produced the protruded lips. It was a most uncomfortable make-up, and a most disagreeable character. I just hated it. The mulatto had a clever but very objectionable mouth. Then, too, it required hours each night, and much soap suds, to get rid of the chocolate color.

Carefully fitted, well made clothes, and the use of small or large pads change the shape of the figure. Unfortunately in my own case my own physical equipment never quite measures up to that of the character I play. I am always either too short and have to use inner soles and heels, or I am too thin and have to pad out here and there, or I am too plump and have to work in vise-like underthings. I do envy the beautiful, young actresses who wear straight make-up in their pictures. That is, a coating of grease-paint and powder before improving the eyebrows, lashes and mouth, just as many women who are not engaged in moving picture acting do. Of course, these actresses are lovely photographic subjects and are endowed with the producer's idea of perfect physical equipment. Then, too, plays are obtained that fit their personalities and type.

THE MAN MAKING UP FOR THE SCREEN

By RAYMOND HATTON

Famous Character Actor

B UILDING screen characters is not, as is the view
of many motion picture players and laymen, largely
a matter of facial make-up. Make-up, of course,
plays an important part in all stage and screen work,
and a thorough understanding of the art of make-up is
essential to all who have ambitions to make a name through
the medium of photodrama.

In a general way, I shall endeavor to explain the function of grease paints. But, first, I shall try to correct the
error most common to screen aspirants: that make-up and
characterization are one and the same thing.

No character in stage or screen history has been or
ever will be a great character because of the make-up that
has been a part of the roles he has played. Make-up is but
a part of screen characterization, and, at the most, a rela-
tively small and inconsequential part.

Make-up—the make-up that counts—the make-up that
makes one's characterizations into living, breathing people—
is below the surface. Characters that have lived for you
when you first saw them, the characters that will always
live in your memory, are the imaginative creations of an
artist's soul. The make-up that you associate with them
has the same importance as the final coat of paint on an
automobile.

Lon Chaney in "Outside of the Law" was the most
Chinese-like Chinaman of the screen that I have ever seen.
His understanding of his role and his sincere feeling for
it resulted in a characterization that approached the perfection for which all of us are striving. Richard Barthel-
mess, on the other hand, in "Broken Blossoms," was equally
convincing, and, because of the nature of his part, more
impressive but with less suggestion of the Orient in his
surface make-up. Perhaps, as I have heard many players

19

say, he would have been more nearly perfect in his interpretation of the lovable yellow man, had he resorted to the use of a realistic make-up. I cannot say. But I do know and feel that it is strikingly significant that one of the greatest character portrayals of stage and screen history was played in what was practically a "straight" make-up.

When I am to assume a character portrayal for the screen, I build my character—put on my "make-up"—my inside make-up—days before I plan to start work on the picture. My character, who is, to me a real, living person, is with me constantly. I study him under all circumstances and he becomes a very concrete and definite thing in my mind's eye. The result, as I see it, is the most natural one. My character develops, grows up, so to speak, and becomes so thoroughly able to take care of himself that he plays his own scenes, while Raymond Hatton, close by, offers an occasional suggestion.

I have a large collection of my characters in my scrap book, but I have a much larger collection waiting to be photographed. Collecting characters is my business; if it had not been my business, it would most certainly have been my chief hobby. Every day I manage to add another to the collection. One I will see on a street car, another at the theatre, others around the studios. These characters have facial lineaments that I must put on the screen through the use of grease paint.

My search for characters that I want for my collection is a constant and unending one. It takes me to strange and often unpleasant places, places that would be quite intolerable to any but a collector such as I am. I have spent many hours in jails with hardened criminals, painful days in hospitals with luckless drug addicts who have given me assistance that I regret I can never reciprocate.

All of these people and many more, whom I have met casually, have added to my versatility as a character actor. Each day I encounter something new to me, something that I have not yet had occasion to transfer to the screen. Experiment, often tedious and trying, follows and continues until I feel that I have accomplished what I set out to do.

Colors play an important part in screen make-up and costuming. It is true that on the film we have only black, white and varying shades of gray. The mere statement of this fact seems simple and to the novice would appear to offer no problem, but illimitable shades of gray tones and the striking effects of each are an endless study to every one interested in producing photodramas.

The subtle differences in the photographic qualities of colors cannot be explained with any degree of accuracy in writing. I could tell you that all red photographs dark and that pale blues and greens are light on the screen, but that would be of little value to you. My purpose in devoting so much of my limited space to color is to impress upon you that you must make a comprehensive study of the subject, if you hope to be successful in motion pictures.

Since I first appeared in photodrama I have been studying color and at the present time my experiments along this line take up much of my time. If I see a player on the set wearing a costume of peculiar or unusual shade or a color that I have never seen photographed, I make it a point to fix the shade definitely in my mind so that I can associate the shade value with its source when I see it on the screen. A man who paints must know colors, and he must know how to blend them, but he has an opportunity to see before him the result as he works,—and he has a chance to correct and change his colors as his painting progresses; a screen actor must know colors. He must know how to blend them, and he must know the photographic value of what he blends. There must be no errors, for he has no chance to correct what he has failed to do correctly the first time.

What I have tried to tell you thus far, though it can hardly be called a guide to make-up, will prove, I hope, a basis for your study of the subject. There is little definite information that I can give which would prove of value to all. The shade of grease paint and powder that a player must use depends on the color of his skin and the general contour of his face. The first and most important function of grease paint is to conceal such imperfections of the skin, often imperceptible to the eye, which would be brought out under the strong lights necessary to good photography.

The basis of every make-up is a grease paint, a thin coat of which is rubbed well into the skin. For a straight character I use a number five, which I can best describe as a rather light brownish-yellow. (This color, however, must not be accepted by any one of my readers as a guide, for, as I have endeavored to explain above, it is impossible to give definite instructions for make-up that will apply to all. What I outline here as my process of making up may be accepted in detail, but each person must determine by experiment the colors best suited to him.) The grease paint, if put on properly, will give the skin a perfectly smooth surface of a shade slightly lighter than the grease appears in the jar. If your skin does not appear normal, except in matter of color, your grease has not been rubbed in sufficiently. Your pores should show as clearly as they normally do before you are ready to go beyond the grease paint.

Above my eyes, in straight make-up, I use a thin, smooth shading of brown. My eyelids are lined with the same color. Many players prefer black for the eyes and never vary from it, but it has been my experience that the brown gives a much softer screen tone which is far more desirable. This again is a matter of personal preference as well as a matter that depends on the natural coloring of the individual, and there can be no set rule.

Many players, even the most experienced, I think, ruin what is otherwise a perfectly splendid make-up by using too heavy color on the lips. My preference is for a rather light red and I use an extremely thin coat of that. In fact, the grease on my lips does little more than accentuate the natural shape of the mouth. The resultant screen tone is a soft dark gray, that suggests the real color of one's lips much more accurately than the hideous black so often seen on the screen. The black, of course, comes from too heavy a coat of too dark a red and is something you should be careful to avoid.

Last, and entirely as important as any other feature of the make-up, is the powder. My powder is a shade that corresponds to the number five paint. Blending powders they are called, and blending powders they should be. The powder covers the entire face and is blended smoothly with the base by the slow and rather tedious process of patting it on gently but firmly with a large powder puff. Choice of color in blending powder and care in applying it is quite as important as any other part of the make-up.

When a person is made up for the screen, his make-up should not be perceptible except in the matter of color. What I mean is that each phase of the make-up should not be considered separately, but as a part of the whole and all must blend smoothly and perfectly.

The details of screen make-up that are best suited to the individual must be worked out by himself. My suggestion to those who have asked my advice is a simple one, but it is effective to those who will work hard and try conscientiously to help themselves. Follow the plan outlined above in a general way, making such changes in color as you think are necessary in your own case. Make careful notes on paper of everything you do so that it would be possible to duplicate the make-up in detail from your notes. When you have completed your make-up to the best of your ability, have a large head photograph of yourself taken. When you receive this photograph, you are ready to begin a serious study of make-up.

You will no doubt be startled by the sight of your first picture in the make-up, but you are sure to find many faults with it if you study it carefully. It is likely that your first attempt will result in a blotchy picture—that there will be large spots on your face darker or lighter than the rest. That would indicate that your make-up was not put on smoothly and that your powder was not blended evenly with your grease paint. Smoothness of make-up is the first requisite. Get that, before you experiment further.

When you are sure that you can put on a smooth make-up, you are ready to study color values. Try a lighter or darker make-up, whichever may seem necessary. This may require three or four more attempts, but persistence will bring results. If possible, show your photographs to an experienced player who will be able to determine your errors in a general way and give you a short cut to what you are striving for. But keep at it, and remember always that you can never learn all there is to know about make-up.

Generally speaking, women use lighter make-up than men. Mrs. Hatton uses a number two grease paint, which is about the average for women in straight make-up, although women must vary their shades of grease with type the same as men. Mrs. Hatton has found after much experimenting that a blend of this number two grease paint with a number seven powder—quite dark—gives the best possible results. Her make-up for her mouth and eyes is quite like mine.

Character make-ups such as I have used in almost all of my pictures are far more difficult than the straight make-up, but the basic principle is the same. You can develope your make-up for characters after you have become master of a straight make-up by following the same course of experiment. You will find that you can make your cheeks appear sunken, if you use a grease on them that will appear darker than the rest of your face. On the other hand you can have the appearance of high cheek bones on the screen, if you make them lighter than your cheeks. Your mistakes—and there will be many of them—in attempting these variations will suggest combinations that will be useful in some other type of make-up.

Character make-up can be developed, as I have suggested, but I would not recommend the beginner to worry too much about it. Except in rare cases, new-comers to the screen play straight parts for a long time before they are assigned to the more difficult character work. In time a player will be assigned to a part that requires some slight variation from his straight make-up, and it is likely that he will play several straights again before he has another. So, by degrees he will learn how to apply character make-up and develop the art of grease paints slowly and certainly.

Many players of experience and most novices are careless with make-up. They try to hurry and put on something that will "be good enough." This, of course, is the worst possible mistake and an inexcusable one. I take at least thirty minutes to put on a straight make-up and a

Raymond Hatton

much longer time for character. My make-up in "The Whispering Chorus," which I think is the most difficult I have ever attempted, took me between three and a half and four hours daily toward the end of the picture, when, you will remember, I had a three-inch scar across my face.

Scars, bruises, cuts, suggestion of broken bones, hare-lips and many other more or less similar illusions are part of make-up, but they are too difficult and too complicated to explain to the novice. These are things that he will learn later, if he starts his motion picture work with the whole-hearted enthusiasm that is necessary for one who is to succeed.

Even the simplest straight make-up can be perfected only after much diligent effort. But that applies, too, to anything that one has an inclination to learn. Pictures are no different. Perseverance will win. Make-up, of course, is an essential to a successful actor—but the big thing is to MAKE UP your mind.

DIRECTING THE PICTURE

Editor's Note: Rex Ingram has distinguished himself by his unusually
fine work in directing such masterpieces as "The Four Horsemen of
the Apocalypse" and "The Conquering Power."

YESTERDAY it was an industry; today it is an art. There, in a nutshell, you have the history of the progress of the making of pictures. As an industry the film might have continued indefinitely to create dividends for investors; as an art, it has become the medium for conveying to the world the message that the great masters of all time have attempted to give us.

Fifteen years have seen the cinema develop from the state where its choicest temples contained but a dozen seats. The public was charged the sum of five cents to enter a nickelodeon, which was disguised as the observation platform of a railroad train, from which they watch a flickering representation of landscape slip away behind them into the distance. It was an illusion obtained by the projection of a motion picture film which had been photographed from the back of an observation car.

Today great theatres, seating thousands of people and containing lobbies which are in themselves as large as an entire legitimate theatre, are devoted exclusively to the presentation of the motion picture. If this remarkable change has come about in the theatres, it is not probable that the development of the cinema, as an art, has remained at a standstill.

It assuredly has not. The motion picture was destined from the beginning to become more important than the legitimate drama because of its tremendous scope. We realize there is no limit to its range when we consider that where one theatre presents a stage play, it is possible for hundreds of motion picture theatres to present identically the same screen production at the same time in all parts of the world.

Hundreds of thousands of people in the civilized world know nothing of the work of Rembrant, Michalangelo, El Greco, Corot and Dore, and would in all probability be little interested in them. Yet, to these people the same message will be brought through the medium of the cinema —the message that the masters of art have given to those of their students who are today engaged in film production.

For the inevitable is coming to pass. Slowly but surely, the cinema is coming into its own, taking its place, if not beside sculpture and painting as an art, most certainly ahead of the spoken drama. The motion picture's unlimited possibilities where sweeping, smashing dramatic effects are desired; the many opportunities it affords to accomplish results not to be dreamt of behind the footlights; the intimacy that can be made to exist between the audience and the characters in the film play—all go to prove that this great new art—until recently termed "industry"—potentially combines that which fine sculpture, fine painting, and the best that the theatre has to offer can give us.

Art is as important as the scope and power of its message. We believe that a fine piece of sculpture which stands in a public square, or part of a city, exerts an ennobling influence upon the citizens. A fine painting that hangs in a public building undoubtedly leaves an aesthetic impression upon those who see it.

We know that our daily lives are greatly influenced by the masters of the spoken drama. Yet, when we stop to consider that for every one person who sees the work of a sculptor, or a painter, for every hundred persons who are present when a spoken drama is enacted—a million or more carry away impressions from the cinema theatres. Just what these impressions are, depends upon the play.

Where sculpture, painting and the legitimate drama belong to the art-loving minority of the nation, the motion picture belongs to the whole people. Therefore, being the most universal, the most easily understood of all the arts, it is bound to take its place in time as the most necessary of them all to a better civilization—going upon the premise that the chief object of art is to exert an aesthetic influence

upon those who come in contact with it and are reached by
its message.

In 1913, when I was studying drawing and sculpture
at the Yale School of Fine Arts, a motion picture play,
founded upon Charles Dickens' famous story, "A Tale of
Two Cities," came to New Haven. It followed in the wake
of many cut and dried one-reel subjects, and while this
picture was necessarily full of imperfections, common to
all pioneer films, it marked a tremendous step ahead in
the making of them.

I left the theatre greatly impressed; absolutely convinced that it would be through the medium of the film play
to the production of which the laws that govern the fine
arts had been applied, that a universal understanding and
appreciation of art finally would be reached. I brought
several friends of mine, most of them either students of the
art school, or members of the Yale Dramatic Association,
the following day to see this picture, which had been made
by the Vitagraph Company of America, and each and every
one of them was as much impressed as I. All of us thereupon
decided to enter the motion picture field. After leaving
New Haven, I lost track entirely of the other members of
that party.

But some months later I was fortunate enough to take
part in a film play, directed by William Humphrey, the
man who had produced this version of the Dickens' story.

As time went on, I began to realize how valuable my
training at the art school was going to prove. In spite of
inattention, I had gained an understanding of the laws that
govern perspective, composition, balance, construction, form
and the distribution of light and shade, thanks to the repeated
lectures on these subjects. And it is through producers
who have acquired knowledge and training of this kind
that the cinema can advance further than all the other arts
in influencing an entirely modern civilization, as only an
art which belongs peculiarly to this day and age can.

Allowing for the difference in medium, practically
the same laws apply to the production of a film play which
has artistic merit, as to the making of a fine piece of sculpture or a masterly painting.

The rough preliminary sketch made in a plastic medium or on paper by the sculptor for his proposed job has its parallel in the synopsis made before the motion picture scenario is blocked out.

Before a scene is taken in a film play, provided ideal conditions exist in the studio, the scenario is completed. For without a well-constructed script, the efforts of the director will fail to convince.

He may have the human note, humor, pathos, fine characterization and photography, well composed pictures and good lighting, but unless he convinces in the telling of his story, all these things stand on a foundation that wabbles.

The sculptured figure or group of figures first takes form in an armature, or firmly constructed frame built according to the proportions of the job. This frame is composed of steel braces, wood and lead piping, all wired together. Upon this structure, the clay is then roughly massed.

Just as the moving picture director must have a thorough knowledge of the scenario construction, the sculptor must be familiar with this part of his work, whether he does it himself or whether it is done for him, for if the armature is unskillfully put together, it will not stand when the great weight of the clay is put upon it, and his efforts will be to no purpose. For even if portions are unhurt when the figure collapses, the mass will not hang together again.

The armature is the sculptor's scenario.

As the sculptor has to compose his grouping, to fit a certain space, on a pediment or a monument, so the director must place his people within given lines, according to the distance they are from the cameras, in order that the massing of figures, the distance, and the arrangement of light and shade will go to make up something that has pictorial value.

However, in this the film often presents a more complicated problem than either paint or clay. The compositions of painter and sculptor are studied out, and when finished remain as their creator left them, but the moving picture composition changes every moment.

Often a fine bit of grouping that has taken the director a long time to compose will be changed to an unbalanced, disconnected mob scene through some alteration in dramatic action. This change sometimes may necessitate an entirely different arrangement of lights, and a different dressing of the set, although in most cases, a different camera set-up or a change of foreground will be sufficient.

There is a tendency in film production when one is striving to make something of beauty, to sacrifice, or lose sight of, the story theme. In moving pictures, this is particularly dangerous. For in sculpture and painting, although the finest examples of both arts have a theme—certainly a meaning—neither are linked so closely to literature as is the screen.

Something rarely sought for on the moving picture screen is form. As with clay and paint, form is one of the most vital adjuncts to the film. Take the close-up for instance. Without knowledge of the construction and forms of the human head it is only by chance that the director can light it in such a way that the modeling is brought out. Lack of modeling will make a head thrown upon the screen appear to be flat and without character, and in doing so weaken the characterization of the player.

It is modeling obtained by judicious arrangement of light and shade, that enables us to give something of a stereoscopic quality to the soft, mellow-toned close-up, which takes the place of the human voice on the screen and helps to make the audience as intimate with the characters as if they had known and seen them constantly in everyday life. Form and modeling help a characterization one hundred per cent.

The most noticeable racial characteristic of the Chinese head is the high, bony structure of the cheeks, a peculiarity that will be accentuated by the source of light coming from above at all times when photographing this particular character. The top light throws a shadow under the prominent cheek bones and gives them a more pronounced effect than could be obtained by any high lighting that a clever make-up artist might use in his efforts to gain this effect.

Sculpture teaches us that color is deceptive. The fact that from a live mask or fine portrait bust of a friend we invariably learn more about the character of the original than we knew before, proves that the theory has something of truth in it. Thus, except in the rare cases when both sculpture and film are colored, the sculptor and director are working in a monotone medium and both are striving for the same result—the one in the round, the other on a flat surface, ánd the director simulates the form which is not there by an arrangement of light and shade calculated to create an optical illusion.

In saying that all arts are kindred we are uttering a platitude. The making of poor pictures is not art just as surely as the modeling an inferior statue or writing of bad music is not art. The big things in all art, we know, are the simple things—those which are stripped of all the pretenses and affectations of the artist.

John Sargent's "Frieze of the Prophets" in the Boston Museum, and the saints in the reredos of the Church of St. Thomas on Fifth Avenue, New York City, by the sculptor, Lee Lawrie, are among the finest examples in America of the splendidly simple thing in art.

In them we see not the surface, but that which lies beneath. When the screen shows us what lies behind the actions in the hearts of those whose reflections are thrown upon it, then it also is accomplishing something toward this end.

What do you think the producers look for in a man when they engage him to take charge of one of their producing units? What qualifications are considered necessary in a successful director? May I tell you?

First, I should say, the ability to create. A broad acquaintance with the world at large; an intimate knowledge of the races; an understanding of how people live in the countries throughout the earth; and the power to visualize the written word in picture form.

You sigh, and say to yourself, "This is indeed a hard profession to break into!" But, I ask you, is it? Would

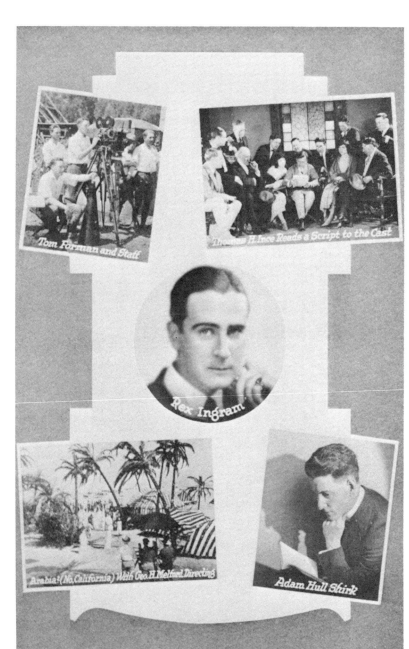

Tom Forman and Staff

Thomas H. Ince Reads a Script to the Cast

Rex Ingram

Arabia (No. California) With Geo. H. Melford Directing

Adam Hull Shirk

it not be equally as hard for one to break into your own profession, whatever it may be, unless one had the training for it? Of course it would. If it were an easy thing to become a motion picture director, the studios would be full of them. It is because it is not an easy thing to become a director, that the work is so attractive. To those unfitted for it, there is no use allowing this work to make an appeal.

The potential director had better be certain that he is a close student of human nature. To make his work stand out and achieve success, it is necessary that the characters he portrays on the screen appear as actual living, breathing persons. One of the surest ways to study human nature at first hand is to mix with all classes of people in all walks of life. Once you are able to do this, you will come to know life, and be able to depict it humanly on the screen.

The director should also be a lover of books. And natural tendency to analyze different dramatic situations will help immeasurably when you are finally qualified to handle the megaphone.

There really is no sure road to the position of director for a motion picture producing company. Some of the rank and file of men and women now directing stars of the screen drifted quite naturally from the legitimate into studio work. Others have served long apprenticeships as actors, writers and cameramen before they were qualified to direct a motion picture.

To know the camera is to know what is possible of it. Therefore a good many of our present day directors have graduated from the ranks of cameramen. First of all they have the knowledge of the limitations or possibilities of the camera. Then they have gained a vast store of information by observing the methods of the various directors when they have served as cameramen.

Since the players are as clay in the hands of the sculptor, as paint at the tip of an artist's brush, it is desirable that, like the artist, the director should have a true sense of art values. He moulds them into the forms desired and called for by the author's script, in one instance, or he places and blends them on his canvas to conform with the story told by the author in another.

THE ASSISTANT DIRECTOR

By SCOTT R. BEAL,

President, Assistant Director's Association, Hollywood, California.

THE assistant director! Ha! now you think, there's a fellow who has very little to do. He's just an assistant. Well, allow me, please, to enlighten you a little about the many and varied duties of the assistant director. Also about the qualifications required to become one.

First of all, he is the business executive of his company. Since this is the case, it is well that you understand something of the method of filming a picture, from the various angles of the work. When you enter a theatre and behold the elaboration of the screen of your favorite story, you are pleased, because, as in the reading of the story itself, the plot gradually unfolds, and your interest in the story is renewed and constantly increases. Probably the author of the story wrote it sequentially, as you recall it, quite differently from the smoothly running motion picture that you see when you go to the movies.

And right there is the story of the Assistant Director and of his duties. In the filming of a motion picture, we will say, for example, that there are twenty scenes, all of which are taken in the same locality, but which, nevertheless, appear in the various reels of the picture and at widely separated intervals. It is, however, necessary in the interests of economy and speed in production, to make all of the twenty scenes at one time, or rather during the one stay in the location where these are all filmed if they are outdoor "shots," or on the same "set" if they are studio "shots." In the former case, there is a great saving of effort, time and expense, in doing all the scenes of a given location at one time. While in the latter instance, where a set takes a considerable space in a studio, it will readily be seen that since studio space is very precious it is imperative that the sets be not allowed to stand a moment longer than necessary.

Therefore it is the duty of the assistant director, first to determine what scenes will be "shot" and to arrange the sequence of the "shooting" of all scenes for the picture in the order in which they should be filmed.

The assistant director is also required to supervise the building of all the sets for the production, and very often to consult with the location man, and determine which of the various locations is best suited to the filming of a certain scene so that the best interests of the story may be maintained.

The assistant director is a lieutenant to the director, and when the director notifies him what scenes he will shoot on the morrow, it is the duty of the assistant, in turn, to notify the players wanted for the filming of these scenes. Very often the assistant director is called into consultation with the casting director to make a selection of various types for bits in the play, or to assist in picking out members for the coming mob scene from the actual "mob" that makes application at the studio for a chance to appear in the film, once the word goes out that a mob scene is to be filmed. He must be a good judge of types and must also understand his director thoroughly. Indeed he must quite often keep that dignitary in a good humor. Which latter bit of information, is of course another "movie secret."

More and more, present-day assistant directors are learning the value of studying the drama. The day is past when the assistant is a sort of office boy to the director. It behooves the aspirant to any work in the moving picture studio to have liberal information about the highest forms of dramatic art, and to keep posted on the workings of every individual part of the great unit known as the studio. When, therefore, the assistant director is in a sense free from his numerous duties he will be found close to the set watching the director at his work, for there is no group of studio workers who should so easily qualify to become directors as the assistant directors.

If you ask just how to qualify for the position of assistant director, I can think of no specific training. I should say that it requires a thorough familiarity with the studio proper, plus dramatic and scenic values. In fact, a great many of the assistant directors are recruited from the ranks of studio workers who have shown peculiar fitness for and adaptation to the intelligent fulfillment of the duties of assistant director. The studio itself is the very best school for the prospective assistant director. If he has an amiable disposition, and is ready to lend a helping hand to any job that may be required of him, whether it comes within his scope of activities in a particular sense or not, or whether or not he is paid for doing something different from his own job, he will probably attract the attention of some director who is on the lookout for such an assistant.

One thing is certain. Once given a position as assistant director, there is a wonderful chance for advancement, and for that reason alone the position should attract men who are desirous of climbing the ladder of motion picture progress by that safest of all mediums, the merits of former achievement. There is little chance of retrogression in the studio. A director does not become an assistant director. Though the reverse is quite possible, and with concentration and tenacity of purpose, more than probable.

The opportunities to become assistant directors are many, since there are very often positions of many kinds open in the studios, and a man has the opportunity to become in time assistant to a prominent director. Once that end is achieved, it is up to the man himself. From there on the path lies straight ahead. Many a path to fame started— indeed as most of them do—in the valley of discouragement, and on the bed-rock foundation of hard work. Just how far up that path one proceeds in the march of progress depends upon the abilities of the individual.

THE CAMERAMAN:
How He May "Break In."

By JOHN ARNOLD,

Member American Society of Cinematographers.

Editor's Note: John Arnold bears the distinction of having photographed every picture that Viola Dana has starred in during the past six years, and it is with great pleasure that we present this chapter to all patrons of the silent drama who may be interested in the opportunity that awaits the cameraman in the motion picture field. Mr. Arnold is an authority on the subject and his views should interest everybody.

T WENTY years ago the motion picture business was really nothing but a toy. Today, however, it is the basis of a business giving profitable employment to thousands of earnest workers. Amusement and education are offered to millions of people, and because of the huge investment of capital involved in the making of motion pictures, the industry at large takes its place as one of the world's greatest industries. Of greatest importance, from the viewpoint of the cinematographer, naturally, is the motion picture camera.

Without it, there could be no motion picture industry. Therefore, it is wise for anyone contemplating breaking into the movies to consider the work of the motion picture cameraman and the possibilities that work offers ambitious and intelligent young men.

With the motion picture camera it is possible to record for everlasting preservation, all important events, so that generations to come may see present-day Presidents inaugurated—the horrors of great disasters depicted and the deeds of great heroes preserved in life-like form so that future generations may see as well as read of the actual events.

All that is interesting in nature, and man's work, in drama as well as in real life, is spread before millions of people in moving panorama because of the eagle eye of the camera lens and because of the cameraman's ability to manipulate that lens.

Therefore, if you are seeking fame and fortune through a motion picture career, and if by chance you happen to have an interest in photography, consider well the possibilities of reaching your goal through motion picture camera work. There is a simple way of illustrating for you the power of the camera.

Do you remember with what glee you hailed the telling of a fairy story in your childhood days? Do you remember how as a child you marveled at the wonderful powers of the fairy godmother's magic wand? How you thrilled with little Cinderella when the magic touch of that wand transformed her into a real fairy queen, and how the pumpkins were instantly turned into splendid stage coaches so that she might attend the great ball in true style?

The feats the fairy godmothers of old enacted with their wands are being rivaled in this modern day by the motion picture cameraman. The motion picture camera is his wand and it is probably the greatest instrument of illusion the world knows today.

Who is best qualified to become a motion picture cameraman? That is not an easy question to answer. I may say, however, that anyone who has demonstrated his ability to make good negatives with the "still" camera could probably qualify with greater ease than one to whom the mysteries of photography are unknown. Upon the cameraman rests the responsibility of getting a good negative of the scene enacted before the camera under the direction of the director. Therefore, it is plain to see that though the director may be particularly qualified to command the players and though the players themselves may be the greatest stars of the silent drama, unless the cameraman is qualified to so manipulate his camera as to register perfectly the action of the scene, all the work of clever directors and splendid players will be for naught.

A photographer, either amateur or professional, capable of making a good "still" picture should be, with a little training, as capable of making a hundred motion picture images of the same scene while the action is taking place. Of course, it is farthest from my idea to attempt to convey the impression that only persons conversant with photog-

"Shooting" a Scene

John Arnold.

Sixteen Camera Men Used to Photograph
"The Four Horsemen of the Apocalypse"

raphy should attempt to become motion picture cameramen. An interest in photography alone is sufficient reason for anyone to consider seriously that department of motion picture work. With interest aroused, there will come the desire to learn and with that desire set in motion, there will come a knowledge of the work and the necessary requirements for success as a cameraman.

Motion pictures gained the full measure of popularity when the cameraman became master of the camera. As soon as the powers of the motion picture camera lens were fully realized and mastered, the motion picture itself took its rightful place in the hearts of a loyal public. Of course, credit must be given to the men and women who studied lighting effects and the many other aids to high-class photography, but, as I see it, the major portion of the credit is due to the man who through his own particular talents is able to give those effects to the public via the screen route and the lens of his camera.

When a dozen years ago the industry was in its earliest beginnings the quality of the films was very poor indeed. They "jumped" and did about everything imaginable to tax the patience of the audience. I well remember our family doctor warning us to stay away from the movies. It was his impression that they would destroy the sight of the eye. It was then that I first became interested in motion picture photography. I was convinced that moving pictures were surely as practical as "still" pictures and once I had entered upon the work I found it of absorbing interest.

When it is considered that less than ten years ago it was difficult at times to distinguish the face of a player, and that now the face of every member of a mob scene is as clear as a close-up, it will be seen that the art of action-photography (as well as the quality of the raw stock) has advanced a thousand per cent. Can you do things in an individual way? Will you try to do something new? Will you investigate every phase of motion picture photography? If so, we welcome you in our branch of picture work. The opportunities to create and make progress in the photographic art are wonderful. A cameraman becomes known by the quality of his work. The same keen efforts that made it possible to show a thousand per cent gain in the art in the last ten years, probably will be apparent ten years from today. What we now consider as nearly perfect work will look mediocre when compared with the effects obtainable at that future time. If you can create, I feel confident that there is room for you as a motion picture photographer.

Of necessity, the expert cameraman must be ingenious. Handed a camera by the manufacturers, it has remained for the cameraman himself to perfect and improve its mechanism so that at the present time the results he is obtaining far exceed the fondest hopes of the camera manufacturers.

Do you love art? Can you appreciate a good picture or drawing when you see one? Do you know why it is a good picture or drawing? Do you understand the principles of composition? That is another quality necessary to camera success. The cameraman is really an artist but, instead of pigments and brushes, he relies upon certain mechanical contraptions designed to take their place. Credit, of course, must be given the director, who is also an artist, but after all it is the director's function only to pose the scene so that he will properly interpret the author's written word picture while it remains for the cameraman to reproduce the scene, adding such photographic beauty as will bring added delight to the millions of pleasure seeking patrons of motion picture theatres.

Nor is the cameraman without his share of credit for what he achieves. If vanity has prompted more people to seek a career in the players' ranks than in the ranks of the cameramen, and if that bit of vanity can be traced to the fact that as players they would see their name in print more often, would it not be well to note that the cameraman is now coming into his own, and that he too is being recognized as one of those who help make screen production possible? It is now the custom to flash his name upon the screen, so that the world at large may know that it was his genius which photographed the picture.

There is another angle from which the motion picture camera must be considered. Its uses are not confined to the studio or research laboratory. Nor are they limited to the field of industrial motion picture making. There are over seventeen thousand motion picture theatres in the

United States. The screens of these theatres have come to be a wonderful medium for the dissemination of the news of the world. How was this accomplished? What makes the screen newspaper, commonly known as the "News Weekly," possible? It is one thing to read your daily newspaper and find recorded there the accounts of events of world importance taking place in every corner of the globe. But it is quite another thing to sit in your favorite movie theatre, a few nights later, and have flashed before your very eyes the actual event.

A better example: a distinguished visitor arrives in your city, circumstances make it impossible for you to journey to the place where he is received, though you really would like to see him personally, and to see how your fellow townspeople received him. You are not quite content to read the newspaper accounts of his reception. But—and this probably has happened to you already—have you not been surprised and pleased to find that that very night during the screening of the regular program in your movie theatre the enterprising manager has attached to the regular "News Weekly" a special pictorial supplement recording every move of the distinguished visitor? How was this done, and who was responsible for it?

There is in the United States today a veritable army of intrepid cameramen who not only understand the essentials of cinematography, but know how to tell a story in pictures. They are located in every large city in the country. The moment an event of importance occurs in their neighborhood they are on the spot with their cameras to "shoot" scenes of the event. It does not matter what it may be. The inauguration of a President, the arrival of a convention delegate— a destructive fire—a great man's funeral—and countless other events occur daily in every section of the country— the members of this army of cameramen are ever ready to make a cinema record of them.

Once the record has been made in film form, the film itself is rushed to the developing room. When the negative has been made, it is hurried to the city where the film releasing companies prepare their "News Weeklies" and if the event depicted is of sufficient importance, it is incorporated in the current "News Weekly" and so reaches the public throughout the world. Of course where purely local happenings are depicted, which would be of interest only to the local population and which are desired to be shown on the day of the occurrence, the cameraman takes his film to the local theatre man, and he simply cements it to the "News Weekly" he is featuring, thus allowing the theatre patrons to view, upon his screen, a photographic record of the day's happening. There you have, then, another angle of the cameraman's activities. And this particular branch of motion picture photography is not limited solely to the taking of news pictures.

With the development of the "News Weekly" a certainty, and with its popularity proven beyond all doubts, there has recently been inaugurated the "Screen Magazine," which depends for its popularity upon the "writer" type of cameraman who can accept an assignment from the producers, or publishers of the "Screen Magazine," and then dig deep into the subject, discover the features that are of real interest, and treat them pictorially so that the theatre audiences may understand them.

If ever there was any doubt in the producer's mind as to the popularity of the "Screen Magazine," it is but necessary to note that what was not so long ago an experiment has become one of the features of many programmes, and is looked for with eager anticipation by an army of ardent screen devotees. Man's natural desire for learning has made this feature so popular. It is probable that the cameraman who succeeds in filming some great educational subject will go down to fame more certainly than the cameraman whose only claim to distinction is the filming of some great star's pictures.

The "Film Reporter" probably does more interesting work than any other class of cameraman. His assignments are varied indeed. One day he may be sent out to meet an incoming vessel, while the next day may find him photographing the President playing golf.

It is truly interesting to contrast the "Screen Magazine" cameraman with his brother photographer working in the studio or on location. There is very little that the studio photographer need worry about. When the director has satisfied himself that all is "set," he gives the order to "shoot." It is the cameraman's duty to photograph the scene which has been painted and set for him by the director. But the "news" photographer has many obstacles with which to contend.

First of all, he must take his picture right the very first time. There are no chances for "retakes." Needless to say, the event he has been assigned to photograph will take place regardless of weather conditions. If it rains or snows he must contend with the problem of bad lighting. Recently a huge building collapsed in the Times Square section of New York City. Every "news" photographer was on the scene before the debris had settled. It was in the early winter season, and the unhappy event took place at dusk. How were the cameramen to take the scenes of this catastrophe which the world would read about the next morning and which the world would see in the "News Weeklies" in a few days?

Still photographs of the scene show the cameramen rigging up a battery of Sunlight Arc Lamps such as used in the studios to provide the intense effect of the sun. Once again the ingeniousness of the cameraman has solved a difficult problem. Here it is, past dusk, and the streets quite dark, and yet the entire scene of the disaster is bathed in a flood of light of equal brilliance to the mid-day sun. Thus it was that the world was able to see the collapse of that building just as if all the millions of eyes that eventually saw it had been focused on the scene.

It is also difficult for the "screen reporter" to "shoot" his scenes. He must make his way through the curious crowds and set up his machine at a point of vantage. Surely "screen reporting" is one of the most interesting branches of the cameraman's work. Anyone with such experience is really qualified to break into the game of taking studio pictures. And the beauty of it is that anyone can become a "screen reporter." All that is necessary is to purchase a motion picture camera and start in. Once you have taken some scenes of real interest, sent them to one of the half-dozen releasing companies specializing in that sort of film material, and if after they view it on their screens they are satisfied that it is of news value, they will purchase it from you, and you may be notified that they would like you to become a regular contributor to their weekly. The photographer is well paid for any negative accepted. Each day that he "grinds" he is securing valuable experience.

If you are thinking of breaking into the movies via the camera route it will be necessary for you to own your own camera, as all cinematographers are expected to own their own machines. Indeed many of the more successful cameramen own a series of cameras, each adapted to some particular use.

It might be well to point out to the amateur cameraman the possibilities that the filming of some important event taking place in his neighborhood really holds. Not so long ago, at one of the Kentucky race tracks, a great turf classic was filmed. The cameraman took the required number of scenes for the news weekly he represented and then went to work and "ground" out many scenes on his own hook. These he turned over to his firm, and recently it was proposed to make a racing picture. Those very pieces of extra negative, depicting the running of the turf classic mentioned above, were found to fit so perfectly the theme of the story that they were the nucleus for one of the successful five reel productions.

One thing is certain: the "newspaper" and "magazine" idea as adapted to the screen is in its infancy. To the cameraman who can create something new in the way of filming and assembling a "screen magazine" there awaits a golden opportunity. It is really the very best way I can imagine for an amateur to break into the game from the angle of the camera. Of course some knowledge of the mechanical workings of the camera are necessary. This, however, will come with its use, and the firm from which it is purchased will be very well able to give the purchaser some lessons.

In summing up, I can say that in the productions of today the cameraman is a big factor; he is the connecting link between the screen folk and the public. Without him there can be no motion picture production. To the earnest worker, willing to spend the required length of time in a course of study and experience, a golden opportunity is open for achievement as a cameraman.

"STILL" PICTURES: HOW AND WHY THEY ARE MADE

By SHIRLEY VANCE MARTIN

Brunton Studios, Hollywood, Calif.

Editor's Note: Shirley Vance Martin probably is one of the foremost "still" photographers in America. His achievements in this department of motion picture work have placed him in the very front rank of his profession, and this chapter, though written in light vein, tells the rather serious story of the "still" in Mr. Martin's inimitable and thoroughly authoritative way.

A SINGULAR title after all, for there are probably not more "stills" in the movies than in other walks of life, even though there has been more written about them. However, this article refers altogether to Still Photography, so the title swings high, wide and handsome and the subject shall be treated with the careless insouciance it generally receives both on the "lot" and outside.

Really, this might be called a little glimpse into that portion of Movieland least often written of, and about which the film habitue seldom hears. The genial press agent gives the fans all the daily dope on the doings of Dotty Dimple, makes the ordinary clerk pop-eyed with envy over the huge salary and earnings of our comedians in funny pants and flap shoes. The ubiquitous publicity man feeds the press daily with anecdotes concerning the culinary, prowess, the sweet simplicity of the domestic life of this charming actress and of the plans and programs of that eminent director. Every point and angle of the game has been served up for the delectation of the dear public except that one angle—perhaps the most interesting of all—that of the "still" cameraman.

In fact, few of those outside looking in know there is such an animal roaming around the movie lot. The very next time you happen to be visiting a studio during the filming of a picture, just ask the first director you meet where you can find the still man. Likely as not he will say, "Oh, him! They keep him chained in a cellar under Stage Six," or something like that, for, while outside the lot such a person is quite unknown and the value and importance of his work scarcely recognized, by the same token inside the fence there are still to be found a few relics of an antediluvian period, who do not recognize and who refuse to be made to realize that upon the skill and resourcefulness of the still man and the excellence of the pictures taken during the making of a film play depend to a very great extent the returns upon the huge fortunes invested in production.

The subject then really deserves our respect, even deference, and yet what does it generally receive? Nine times in ten "the organization" is built, headed, of course, by The Finances, then Production Manager, Director, stars, cameraman, etc., on down the vanishing perspective, until away at the very tip end of the dog's tail is one little flea—that's the still cameraman.

It is a fact that many directors even now consider that little flea a pest and would annihilate him with one crack, while as a matter of fact the still man's work is as truly essential to the success of the picture as that of the director himself.

Still pictures are made for the publicity department to place in magazines for advertising in trade journals and papers, to shoot to the releasing agencies. Even though a film has been disposed of through such an agency, it has to be sold to the dear public after it has been sold to him. It is self-evident that the finer the quality of the stills and the more truly they depict the dynamic moments of a play the keener the competition among the exhibitors to show the film, and—well, really and truly now, dear fanette, just what is it that takes you to the little Star Picture Palace week after week? You and your girl friend pass the much decorated lobby and its "Oh, Edna, let's see what's on this week!" and you consult what—the program? No, Ma'am. You look at the still pictures on display and if they are full of pep and lots of love and a hundred and fifty feet of kisses it is a copper riveted cinch—you are going to that show. And you go *because* you like the stills. Am I right? Or, about half right anyway—the other half being that you just had to see your very most favorite idol? And at that you found him first—in the stills—making perfectly grand love. Again, am I right? You're right, I'm right.

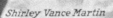

Outdoors Still Photography

Shirley Vance Martin

Indoors Still Photography

Did you know that stills are printed literally by the thousands for you? There is one actress who has mailed at one time twelve thousand pictures, character studies, of herself. She maintains a complete department for the work, well knowing the value to herself of still pictures, frequently placing single orders of 50,000 and 100,000 prints from one negative, all to be sent to admirers. And as for the Handsome Hero, nearly all of them keep a secretary who maintains a filing system, indexed, crossed and double-crossed, of the names of ardent ladies who write for his latest picture in "The Busting of a Bleeding Heart." These still pictures create an interest in both person and play, obtainable in no other fashion, and should publicity photographs be poor in photography and cheap in workmanship the popularity of that particular actor would receive a setback absolutely certain to be felt at the box office.

Ask any old hard-boiled publicity man and see what he says. He is always howling his head off for good stills and likewise howling the still man's head off if they are not good, for *he* knows the financial value of the very best work obtainable. One of the keenest directors in the business used to call his still photographer "George Stillman, the Human Pest." And was George ever given time and opportunity to use his knowledge of composition, lighting, balance, etc., etc.? He was not. It was "Hey, you, George Stillman, pop in there quick and get that. Hurry now. 'Ryou through? Hurry up, gosh ding it, what's holding yuh, anyway?"

The movie cameraman has had hours of consultation with director, electrician and technical man, and to work out and plan his composition and lighting effect; has miles of film on which to picture his action, letting it reach climactic effect in proper sequence. But George is given about 90 2-3 seconds to lug in his heavy box, set up to best advantage, take infinite pains to get the heroine always beautiful, throw a becoming back light on the strong, manly profile of the leading man, place his plate, grab the action by the tail, yell for lights and Bing! and get out. Next morning he is expected to hand in a veritable *Detaille* or *Verstchagen* in beauty of detail and dramatic action. Sometimes the results embody exactly the very effects Mr. Director had in mind.

Does he go over and, smoothing the classic brow of George Stillman, compliment him on his clarity of vision and perfection of technique? Yes, he doesn't. He probably says, "M-m hm hm, yeh that's my stuff!"

Just the same, George Stillman has had many a chuckle since making the discovery that every man jack on the lot—producer, director, leading juvenile and on down the list—likes to see himself or herself in the stills and when the daily "take" is handed in, does Mr. Director look for "action"; does the technical man look to see how his pet scene photographed? No! He flips the prints through to see his own phiz smiling up at him, and if George Stillman has been hep to his job, Mr. Director finds himself in one or more graceful poses. It's human nature. We all like it. But do you ever see one single picture with the still man in it? *Jamais, jamais de la vie.* In more than 400 still pictures taken in "KISMET," not one was taken including Mr. Stillman's handsome map. Can you beat it? I ask you.

Interesting problems to solve by hair-trigger judgment are of daily occurrence. Seldom are the many lights, placed for the movie camera, exactly suited to the still camera, and they have to be quickly and effectively changed—broad and hard, with heavy shadows for strong action, or so daintily graded for a close-up as to completely satisfy that most exacting of all human beings, a movie star. The youthful must be kept youthful, and the one not so young must be made to look younger. And woe betide the still man who, by improper arrangement of lights, gives even a hint of a double chin—male or female. That is the crime de luxe, and is punished by "eternal fire."

The still cameraman is of necessity a versatile flea. He cannot simply bite the dog on the end of the tail. He must bite him all over. First, of course, he must be a good photographer, not only a good photograph maker, but a good still photographer—there are many movie cameramen who cannot explain the first principles of still photography. Portraiture, composition, optics, chemistry, a thousand technical details enter into the daily problems to be worked out swiftly and surely; every moment of the play must be followed, the climaxes mentally registered in detail that they may be instantly built up again and caught before the actors get out of character and before the action gets cold.

That quick thinking and deftness of action are most essential is easy to believe. During the recent filming of "The Queen of Sheba," the writer was called upon for special portraits of the little queen. A scant two and a half hours were given for the work, but in that time more than fifty portraits, each carefully and accurately posed and draped, were made, lights changed to accentuate the young lady's beauty, and three changes of costume made. They were corking pictures, too. The lady herself said so, and that tells a lot.

Perhaps our flea's one greatest requisite, after being able to do everything else on the lot, is to be tactful. Only by having a fund of genuine diplomacy, either born or beaten into him, can he get the best out of those around him; without it he may get good photographs, yes; but great photographs, no.

Besides taking portraits and shooting the action, the still cameraman's ordinary duties include the photographing of every character in the cast for a record of costumes, make-up, jewelry, etc. Scenes are shot weeks apart, which in the finished film appear in continuity, so every character must have minutest details to follow, without depending upon memory. The recording of stage settings with all furniture and props in place, testing of color schemes, both in costumes and scenes, copying prints and illustrations in books at the libraries, picturing street scenes which may have to be reconstructed, all combine to make his day a fairly active one.

The recent play "KISMET," with Otis Skinner in the stellar role, gave the writer wonderful opportunity for dramatic effect in the still pictures, and the magnificent scenic investiture of that Arabian Knight's dream lent itself fully to rarely beautiful effects, both in lighting and composition. At no time in all the nine weeks consumed in transferring the fantastic tale to a film ribbon was there a moment which was not full of interest. Once in the prison scene, when the beggar recognizes his ancient enemy and creeping over in the dusty half-light strangles him with those marvelously expressive hands, all on the stage were literally enthralled, thrilled to silence with the intensity of the moment. Tony, the cameraman, broke the string, exclaiming, "In all my life this is the first time I was so carried away I forgot to crank!" Always when Mr. Skinner was on the stage, the picture impulse ran high and hundreds of photographs might have been made, running the full gamut of his emotions. One particular portrait made rapidly on the set, in perhaps 120 seconds, he complimented very highly as being the best ever taken of him in costume.

"Location tomorrow," is the call which stirs the blood of every member of the company, but most of all the still man, for usually "location" means the mountains, the big woods, the picturesque rocky sea-coast, nearly always some spot of beauty where his picture sense may be given full play and his fancy free rein.

In one play, "location" was up among the big pines in the heart of the San Jacinto mountains, picturesque beyond my feeble powers of description; range after range of purpled mountains, tumbling brooks, waterfalls, a lake of exquisite beauty; nature giving everything to the cameraman as his very own. Small wonder his heart is in each picture made in such surroundings. On this same trip were several mornings of dense, cold fog—a hundred feet away and one was lost. However, with all hands muffled to the ears and all cameras shrouded to the very lenses to keep out the wet, many scenes were shot in the mist—weird, uncanny figures creeping into view and gone again into the fog almost instantly. "It's never been done before in the pictures," quoth the assistant director. This fog business was not in the scenario as written, but since it was forced upon us, it was used; and let me say that when we returned to the studio, 150 miles or so from our mountain location, we reproduced that same fog effect perfectly with the sun brightly shining. That everything is possible in the movies is trite. but certainly and wonderfully true.

Among other duties, the still man has to keep his mental eye peeled for publicity stuff—off stage glimpses of actor, director, the mechanics of the movies, any bit of the game which might be of interest to the outside world. The director, the villain, the pulchritudinous hero and the dainty heroine, "executing" Mme. Butterfly, give us an intimate view of the family in a moment or two of relaxation.

Standing astraddle the rafters, 40 or 50 feet above the stage, in the effort to obtain a publicity view of a ballroom with three hundred or four hundred people, lights, mechanics, etc., is hardly considered a stunt by George Stillman. Airplane stuff is all in the day's work. Nevertheless, the hop-off seldom fails to give a thrill and it gets exciting when, strapped in the cockpit, camera wired and guyed fast, you fly up and up, then suddenly feel a surge against breast and shoulder straps, find your head where your feet ought to be—toward the earth—and a picture to take.

Somehow, George gets the shot though, and once more on solid ground scarcely thinks the stunt worth mentioning. A real thriller of a feat was to be lowered off a precipice in a rope swing with hundreds of feet of mere atmosphere below. To shoot a still of a movie stunt picturing action at the mouth of a mine, I have perched on a mountain ledge, head under the dark cloth facing the mountains and my coat tails exactly a thousand feet from the nearest place to sit down.

Some of the incidents in George's daily existence are highly humorous and lend spice and a certain variety to his otherwise dull existence. As, for instance, the time when on duty at a "rodeo" a husky steer, about the size of a couple of mountains and with a perverted sense of the funny, made for George Stillman and the camera—head down and tail up. When he made his first move, George was looking in the camera; when he moved next, George was in the distant perspective, almost, I may say, at the vanishing point, and the camera was distinctly on the horns of the dilemma. Everybody laughed but George, and that one time he didn't get the picture.

Only once in a long camera career has he wished to be a coal heaver, or to hold some other artistic position which would keep him always on dry land. In a Jack London play, at sea for some ten days, all went well—when the sea was calm—but when we struck the open ocean and the gentle zephyrs got all snarled up, every soul was wholly miserably ill. In some fashion, the scenes were shot with the movie camera while the still man lay limp in the lee scuppers, or whatever they were. When George Stillman was called, he got to his trembling pins, green of eye and gray of face, pressed the bulb feebly and lay calmly down in his beloved scuppers to die, and wondered why he didn't. But he got his pictures.

The necessity for a still man of experience and ability in each separate working unit is being recognized to a greater degree every day. In fact, each production with any aspiration to greatness either pictorially or box-officially, carries a still man who is considered as essential a part of the personnel as director, movie cameraman or electrician. Hobart Bosworth's still man is an artist—I use the word with all due discretion—and his pictures are marvels of technical beauty. The unique production of "The Rubiayat" demanded the services of one of the finest photographers we know of. Mr. Alan Dwan has but recently brought from New York a famous photographer for special still work at a huge salary. William Fox has written at length upon the value and importance of still pictures. The Jackie Coogan Productions have gone to a great length in the quality of the still pictures of the wonderful boy, taken during the first picture under his own company management. Bound editions of portrait studies made at immense cost have gone forth for·publicity purposes.

The old day of the haphazard method of letting "props," the cameraman's assistant, or any other old body, expose a few plates and call them still photographs, is past. The Finances as well as the Exhibitors are rapidly becoming acquainted with the fact—as true five years ago as it is now that the flea on the tip of the dog's tail is as necessary to the dog's happiness as the waggin' tail itself—that the still pictures do their large share in the successful exploitation of the film, just as do star, director and cameraman. So it truly seems to be that our still man is slowly, but surely, to come into his own, his talent recognized and his work rewarded as it should be.

THE ART DIRECTOR—HIS DUTIES AND QUALIFICATIONS

By MAX PARKER

Chief of the Art Staff, Famous Players-Lasky West Coast Studios

R ALPH WALDO EMERSON has said in one of his essays that one-half the world does not know how the other half lives. His meaning is as truly applicable to the industries of mankind as to their social life. Few men are initiated into the mysterious crafts of industries other than those with which they are intimately associated. More particularly true is this, when an industry, by its needs and limitations, is confined to a comparatively small specific basis.

Such an industry is the production of motion pictures, and the studio is, in the last analysis, only a busy factory. Yet around the many activities which enter into the making of motion pictures, a skein of mystery has been woven. Possibly the one phase of studio work which most rarely reaches the attention of the picture enthusiast, and about which gathers the most erroneous ideas, is the work of the men in the studio Art Department, the spinners of the backgrounds on which the gossamer threads of fancy are embroidered.

Perhaps you have realized that before a story can be enacted and photographed, a setting or background must be provided. The design, the supervision and the erection of these settings comprise the work of the Art Director and his staff of assistants.

Briefly, their work falls into two general classifications: First, the creation or design of settings in chartcter or period styles, which while created to suit the requirements of the story's action, are so actually typical that they might exist; next, the duplication or reproduction of certain existing structures called for in the story, so exactly executed that persons intimately acquainted with the original will be unaware of the artifice.

As art director of the Hollywood studio of the Famous Players-Lasky Corporation, I entered motion picture work after more than fifteen years of active architectural practice, embodying almost every phase of design and construction. One important item among the other experiences in this training was the design and construction of exposition and fair buildings.

This training was peculiarly advantageous, for of all the work that an architect is called upon to do, the design of fair buildings requires perhaps the greatest architectural vision and imaginative talent, because such buildings, particularly those for the amusement concessions, usually have no precedent, and are purely the children of a creative brain.

After such experience, I came into the studio almost as an apprentice, and there still remained ahead of me a colossal amount of study and research before I could qualify as a competent art director's assistant. Five years of practice and study prepared me to accept the responsibilities of an art director and assume charge of this department.

Our Art Department at the studio has at all times a staff of from four to six skilled architects and a clever and accomplished artist. The work of these men, while fascinating in its variety, is also difficult and exacting.

Some idea of the scope of the work may be gained by the reflection that motion picture stories have turned back Times pages to every period of the world's history, have traced their characters to every known land and sea on the face of the globe—and often to lands that never were and never will be, that exist only in the vision of the story teller.

In some countries, such as Italy, France and England, the style of architecture, decoration and its kindred arts, has varied greatly during the periods of the country's history, and these variations in design are called the period styles. In other countries, such as China and Japan, there has been but slight variation throughout their entire history, yet the elements of construction and design are quite distinct from those of any other locale, and are classed as character styles.

Our domestic architecture is a composite of borrowed period and character style, as well as some mongrels which

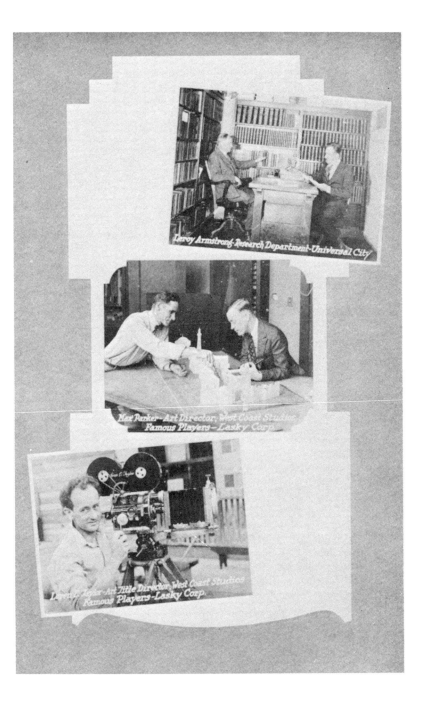

Leroy Armstrong—Research Department—Universal City

Max Parker—Art Director, West Coast Studios
Famous Players—Lasky Corp.

Dwight Taylor—Art Title Director, West Coast Studios
Famous Players—Lasky Corp.

defy any attempt at classification, and which for want of a better name are classed as "East Brooklyn," "Eastlake," "Tenement Stuff," etc., and yet which differ widely in detail. The structures of the Colonial period in America, while they possess influence and elements in common, differ widely according to their locale. For instance, the Colonial houses of New England are quite easily distinguishable from those of Virginia and the South.

So the locale of a story may be entirely identified by the character of the settings; the time or period by the style of design. So, too, in the case of a residence, the position in life of its occupant, his character, moods and peculiarities.

Therefore this staff of architects must be exceptionally versatile, and able to identify by settings any corner of the world and any period of history at a moment's notice. In addition to this, they must be versed in every angle of production, understanding camera technique, lighting and the craft of the artisans who will execute their designs. A final requisite, perhaps the one most important, is the capability for speed. For in a motion picture studio every unit must work with machine-like precision, and no part can fail in its functioning without delaying the entire production and entailing a great monetary loss. In each picture there are from five to twenty-five settings, and from four to nine companies in production almost constantly. This means that where the average architect is able to spend weeks in the evolution of a design, the work of the Art Department is limited to a few hours or days, and construction must follow quite as rapidly.

And yet, every day, I am the recipient of applications for positions from persons who are really untrained, and who have an idea that they possess a talent which unfortunately has not yet been developed. The men we need are men who have had their training, and who, when given work to do, can jump at it and turn the designs out at top speed—and when I say work, I do not mean the sketching of a bungalow or a pretty face or the careful rendering of a flower, but the design of buildings of all classes; streets, entire villages even, of every character and in any part of the world. You can see that this is not a

school for cub draftsmen. Nor can we spend the time to
find out whether or not a man has a talent that can be
developed.

After a story has been accepted for production and the
continuity written, the work of the Art Department begins.
A copy of the continuity for every story is furnished the
art director and he studies with his staff very carefully the
requirements of every scene. Say the story has for its locale
Afghanistan, and in scene No. 215 the action calls for a
native village street. The hero, pursued by the villain, rides
into the scene on a racing camel, and lifting his lady from
a balcony on which she is waiting, rides out through a gate
at the end of the street.

How high is the camel? And where will that balcony be
placed so that the action may be carried out? In conference
with the director, the art director learns exactly how the
former has visualized the scene and approximately where he
wishes the major action in relation to the camera; where he
desires entrances and exits and the nature and massing of the
subordinate or atmospheric action planned, such as mob
movements, merchandising and trading.

All such questions must be clearly understood before
work can commence on the set and the director be assured
that it will be ready for him at a specified time. Once the
requirements of the set have been established, the art
director instructs members of his staff as to these requirements, the approximate size and the placing of such buildings as will be used, their use, the angle at which the camera
will view the set and the distance at which it will be placed
from the foreground in the long shots.

The architect has probably never been in Afghanistan,
and so consults the Research Department, from which he
secures every available photograph or written description of
the country. He may find a picture in which there is shown
a balcony that may be adapted to the action of the set; if
not, such a balcony must be designed along with the building
upon which it is placed.

He studies the methods of construction, the materials
used, the motifs of architectural design and detail until he

is thoroughly familiar with Afghanistan and the Afghanis-
tanese way of doing things. He may read descriptions of
street life in the country, of the bazaars or stalls that line
these streets.

He then begins the scale and detail drawings, plans and
elevations of the buildings that form the street, using—or
simulating where it is not possible to use—the materials
used in native construction. He duplicates native ornament and detail in full sized drawings. These drawings
are blue-printed and a copy furnished to each of the departments that will co-operate in the construction, exactly as the
architect who designs your house will make drawings and
supply copies to each of the contractors involved.

Often, in the case of a complicated, or very elaborate
setting, a scale model will be constructed of cardboard and
other materials so that the director will be able to see clearly
the background that will be given him before construction
is started.

A few years ago, the methods used in building sets were
largely borrowed from the stage, walls being crudely constructed of canvas and depending upon the scene painters'
ability at faking for any semblance of substance and reality,
often windows and doors and even furniture being merely
painted. Today the entire process has advanced in keeping
with the other phases of the motion picture art, and settings
are built substantially and of genuine materials, designed not
only to be correct and appear as a reality, but to enhance
the artistry of story and acting with beauty in line, mass
and balance. I am confident that the motion picture setting
has the possibility of being and in fact often is a potent factor in the education of a great mass of people, bringing to
them painlessly and effectively a new sense of beauty in
architecture and decoration, that will react as a stimulus
toward civic improvement and the bettering of their surroundings.

A completely equipped mill and carpenter shop con-
structs all woodwork and erects a frame. If there are plas-
tered walls they are executed by artisans in that line. If
there is work supposedly in stone, such as columns with

their bases and capitals, friezes and cornices, or carved panel work, skilled sculptors execute these in clay according to drawings, imitating even the texture of the stone that would be used. A mould is made from the model, and the pieces are cast in plaster. If there is carved wood used in the construction, an experienced wood carver executes this.

The painters, when the carpenters and others have the set erected, come in with their colors and apply the finish; when it is necessary they supply the stains and weathering of time and other agents. It must be remembered that while the sets are painted and decorated in color, on the screen these appear only as some tone of gray. In painting for the camera, therefore, the actinic or photographic value of color must be considered in order to secure the proper contrast of light and dark surfaces, inasmuch as a yellow or orange photographs quite dark, while a blue—which is to the eye much darker—will photograph very light.

After the painters have finished, the set is ready for the decorators or set dressers, and in the case of exteriors, the gardener. The "set dressers" furnish the set in character, supplying from the immense property warehouse or from outside sources the hangings, utensils, ware and trappings or furniture required.

Here also care must be exercised to obtain accuracy, lest in the case of your street in Afghanistan, a man who has been there may provide the producer or the press with material for scathing denunciation, by informing the universe that one of the extra mob in the street scene carried a shillalah, unknown in Afghanistan.

This entire preparation the art director in most studios does, and should, supervise, until the set is ready to turn over to the director. He must be able to foresee any difficulty in securing the desired action, or any difficulty in the photography, as well as any error or inconsistency in design and decoration; and he must correct the same before it has been registered by the camera.

Practically the same procedure as described for a street in Afghanistan is followed in the design and construction of every setting, exterior and interior, called for in the continuity of a picture. Of course, in the use of domestic architecture not quite so much research is necessary, and yet the Art Department subscribes to all the best architectural periodicals, keeping in close touch with the work of the foremost American architects and the most modern expressions of beauty in design.

Where it is necessary to reproduce an existing structure, the architect works from photographs in much the same manner, his first problem being the establishing of a scale whereby he can measure accurately the size of every article used in the construction of the original. The effect of perspective in photographs complicates this problem greatly. Recently at the Lasky studio the lobby of the St. Francis hotel at San Francisco and a fountain in the Luxembourg Gardens of Paris have been reproduced.

In a modern and domestic story, it is not always necessary to build every exterior, as the exteriors of apartment houses, residences, public and similar buildings may be found in the vicinity of the studio, permission for the use of which may be obtained from the owners. The Location Department, as it is called, maintains a very complete cross index of such places, as well as a list of places where the natural scenery is similar to or typical of some specific locality. Truckee, California, certain times of the year presents almost perfectly the illusion of the far north country; Guerneville, on the Russian river, has scenery that corresponds with the scenery of some of the French Canadian provinces.

It is not always possible, however, to find a "location" that is suitable and available. Some months ago, after an exhaustive search for a lumber camp such as was called for in the script, it was ascertained that no such camp was at that time in existence. With a notice of one week, the Art Department was instructed to build on the stage an entire and complete lumber camp in the heart of the pine woods, which would tie in with and match other shots photographed in such woods on location. No small job, and yet within a week, such a camp had been built, complete to the slightest detail, and as the story was flashed on the screen the actors apparently walked from one section of dense forest directly into their cabins in camp. In reality the two sections were hundreds of miles apart, one an actuality, the other built upon a stage. And thus we fool the public.

Where an exterior is photographed "on location" the interior may be built at the studio, making it necessary not only that both correspond in physical features such as door and window openings, but to tie up in character and style the built interior and established exterior, although this interior is not at all the same as that of the existing building, but created to suit the action of the story.

To explain: View the picture sometime in which a character is shown approaching the exterior of some building, which he enters. As the camera cuts to the interior, do the doors and windows seem to occupy the same relative positions inside as they did outside?

If they were casement windows outside, are they French windows inside? Is the character of the architecture and decoration inside what you have been led to expect? It would be obviously inconsistent for a character to enter a stone mansion and find himself in a cow shed, and yet some of the inconsistencies that have been seen on the screen as the result of faulty design of settings are, while not so glaring, equally ridiculous to a person of intelligence. Fanciful settings, such as the setting for a fairy tale episode, trick and effect stuff, furnish wide play for the imagination of the Art Director and his assistants. They demand, also, an immense amount of ingenuity and inventiveness. Full grown men are made to appear the size of children by the application of well known laws of proportion.

In making "The Little American" a picture, with Mary Pickford as the star, it was necessary to depict the sinking of the Lusitania. You can readily imagine what it would mean to attempt to do this in mid-ocean, the cost in dollars and cents, and the lives endangered. Such a thing was out of the question. Therefore, we did it in the studio. It meant the construction of an immense reinforced concrete tank, of a size adequate to contain a structure which was an exact duplication of that ill-fated ship. There were shots both inside and outside the hull, which conveyed to the audience that the vessel was indeed upon the high seas. After the torpedo struck, the whole structure listed with terrifying realism and was flooded with a torrent of water. The effect was gained and yet it would take a prohibitive amount of space for me to attempt to convey to the reader an idea of the tremendous amount of study and calculation necessary to create that effect.

Cinderella ballrooms of plate glass and mirrors, the palace of the Snow Queen with a vast skating floor of real ice supplied by a specially installed refrigeration plant and with a weirdly wonderful aurora borealis, water fetes with gorgeous dining barges and swan boats, entire theatres with their auditoriums, stages and dressing rooms, English baronial castles and even the war vault of the former Emperor of Germany with its fiendish and inhuman instruments of murder, follow in kaleidoscopic variety in the vast web of backgrounds.

Every day brings a new problem and a new corner of the world to the attention of the Art Department. They may well be called "the stay-at-home travelers" of the studio, for they often work in four or five countries in the course of a single week. To the Art Director and his staff the phrase "it can't be done" does not exist. "It must be done, and in a helluva hurry!"

If, after reading this outline of the duties, trials and tribulations of one already experienced in and engaged in the motion picture Art Department work, you weigh in your mind your own qualifications for handling the work, you feel consciously that you are capable—then look for a job. But just remember that you are one in a thousand, all similarly confident and with the same chances.

Of all the activities in the motion picture industry, I call to mind one that demands more exacting preparation, greater talent and experience than is demanded of the members of the Art Department. You may have worked in an architct's office and thought you worked hard and fast, but you do not know what hard work and speed mean until you get into the pictures.

ART TITLES

By LOREN E. TAYLOR

Chief of Art Title Department, Famous Players-Lasky West Coast Studios

Editor's Note: Loren E. Taylor heads this department at the Lasky Studio. Mr. Taylor became interested in this phase of the industry and enthusiastic over its possibilities in the early days of motion picture production. He foresaw, then, the vast effort that would some day be attached to this line of endeavor, and with the same clear vision he has succeeded in building a department that would take care of the need as the industry grew.

ONE-HALF of the film footage of the average photoplay is devoted to titles. Ponder, then, over the volume of work that falls to the Art Title Department, in a studio where some millions of feet of film are turned out in photoplays each year.

The titles used in a photoplay, like the settings, may be divided quickly into two general classifications. First, the main titles, which include the producer's mark of manufacture, as well as the credit title, in which credit is given to the director, the author and others directly responsible for the production. Second, the subtitles. The subtitle may again be classed as explanatory and spoken. The explanatory titles are those which cover, in a few words, those elements of the plot that would be long-drawn out or obtuse if reduced to action, or that cannot be conveyed except by the written word.

In the evolution of language, words have come down as the symbols of objects and ideas. Writing is the science of employing these symbols so that they may recall, to the one who reads, either an object or an idea. In the photoplay, where the story must progress swiftly to its conclusion, it is essential that these written explanations convey their idea as quickly as possible to an audience composed of persons of every degree of intellect and perception. It has therefore become the custom to supplement or enlarge upon the written word with a picture of the object or objects associated with the idea.

Wealth is an abstract idea associated with money or gold, and so, on a title which explains that a character is wealthy, a drawing of a vast pile of gold or money by association more vividly brings the idea to the mind of one who reads. This is a practical application of the psychology of suggestion.

To the imagination and skill of the artists in the Art Title Department is due the success of this purpose. The artists in the studio are of many sorts. Some of them are specialists, some versatile, all of them exceptionally talented. We have landscape artists, portrait artists, artists who are experienced in the rendering of architectural perspective, commercial artists with engraving house experience. Some are artists with a genius for the portrayal of Western subjects, some picture animals in motion, and some do only still life. We have also men who do nothing but hand lettering. These arists have had all the way from fifteen years', to thirty-five years' experience in their work, yet we receive applications from all over the world from the students of art and persons who have an idea that they are natural born artists, and have never been given a chance to try their talent.

Judging from the use to which Art Titles are put, one can readily see how vast is the field of subjects in which these artists work. And, in addition to this, their work is further complicated by the photographic values of colors. Remembering that all colors photograph as shades of gray or black, you will see that the artist must know exactly what color value to use in order to create on the screen the proper balance of light and shadow. To illustrate, say that an artist wishes to draw a brick wall on which is growing English ivy. To the eye, the green of the ivy is darker than the red of the bricks. But to the camera, the ivy would be of a lighter shade than the wall. These artists, because of this, work almost entirely in monochrome, and it takes an artist with a great imagination and talent to reduce to monochrome his conception of the idea expressed.

There are some exceptions to the rule, however. By a patented process of color photography, we are producing Art Titles in natural colors.

The Art Title Department is supplied with a copy of the continuity, containing the titles that are necessary to the unfolding of the story. These titles are set up in type and printed by a special process onto cards. The artists are then assigned their work, and proceed to work out drawings that fit the idea conveyed in the title.

When this drawing, or more properly, painting (for the artists work usually in oil, pastel, or opaque wash), is completed, the printed title and the painting are photographed on the same film.

The printing equipment of the Title Department is of the most modern and efficient type, and only master craftsmen are employed. Here, also, the printed inserts which are used in photoplays, such as billheads, newspaper articles or entire newspapers, cards and labels, are made. Special camera equipment also is used in the photographing of titles, and is operated by a cameraman who is a specialist in this work.

It would be well for ambitious amateurs, reading this, to realize that the Art Title Department is not by any means an art class, and unless a man comes to me with a world of EXPERIENCE, proven ability and keen imagination as well, he will not be considered as an applicant.

THE MOTION PICTURE LABORATORY: HOW IT OPERATES

By LEWIS W. PHYSIOC

Laboratory Superintendent, Goldwyn Pictures Corporation

FEW people seem to understand the functions of the laboratory. They visualize it as a place where proceedings of deepest secrecy go on. On the contrary, I believe that if the public did understand the scope of the laboratory where the films they so eagerly view are made, they would have a keener appreciation of the art of the silent drama.

Every now and then, I receive letters from aspiring amateurs who would like to break into the movies from this end of the business. So few seem to understand the qualifications for admittance as an employe of the motion picture laboratory, that I think it would be well for me to enumerate these qualifications.

First of all, it is my firm belief that the laboratory offers the ambitious person a wonderful opportunity to gain a reputation for himself, inasmuch as it is in the laboratory that many of the wonderful effects noted on the screen are obtained. A great deal can be done in the laboratory, in the way of printing effects—such as double exposures, fades and dissolves—that are found necessary after the negative is developed, and that will make for wonderful effects on the screen.

To the man or woman willing to study the photographic printing art from the bottom rung of the ladder, there is an opportunity to break into the movies in this highly interesting branch of screen work. If the aspirant has some technical knowledge of the developing process of the ordinary "still" negative he will probably be better qualified than if he knows nothing of the work at all. However, if the applicant has intelligence and an aptitude for chemical problems he will soon make headway in the film laboratory, though, of course, it must be directly understood that there are no open arms waiting to welcome an amateur in these advanced days.

Here is a short history of the laboratory routine and equipment, its achievements in the past and its possibilities for the future.

Upon the hypothesis that certain periods of time produce certain developments or demonstrations of a particular art, we have every reason to believe that time will unfold the highest manifestation of moving picture genius, as well. Just now, the possibilities seem limitless.

A resumé of motion picture developments leads us into the observation of a department little exploited, as a working function of the enterprise. Doubtless many do not know of its existence. This is the motion picture laboratory, than which there is no more essential department in the industry. Yet in comparison with the other branches, this department has progressed more rapidly than the other technical departments.

Take the camera; barring one or two improvements, it is almost the same as the camera of earlier days, except for the matter of the various devices which have been added from time to time at the suggestion of the cameraman— which slight alterations have not materially changed the instrument.

The cameraman solved only the first problem of the art—that of making the exposures. It remained for the laboratory to accomplish the greater feat of developing and printing from these negatives thousands of feet of film, upon which depended the success of the investments involving stupendous sums of money.

Inventive skill is the outcome of patient experimenting. In the constant daily triumphs over small obstacles lies the real growth and progress of a profession or trade. The motion picture laboratory is no exception in this regard.

In the pioneer days, crude hand machines, of the step or intermittent type, exposing but one frame at a time, were employed to print these films. About eight pictures per second was the maximum of speed, other points of the machine moving correspondingly slowly. In those days, the limit of capacity was about four or five thousand feet per day. Moreover, the negatives were unfit for use after a very few copies had been made. With the "cutting" of scenes into reels it became necessary to attach motors to the printers in order to speed up maneuvers. More changes and greater improvements were inevitable.

Under the old method, each scene was printed separately, or just as often as copies were needed. So many joints were occasioned by the splicing together of these copies in their proper sequence was very slow and irksome business. This difficulty was augmented by the introduction of the "cut back" and short scene—often but a few feet in length—and necessitated the joining of negatives into rolls of about 200 feet, from which the positive was printed in this length, all in one, thereby reducing the splices from 100 or more to five or six. Then there was the new difficulty of having several scenes of varied density in one roll of negatives. When given the same exposure in printing, the result was anything but desirable.

To counteract the difference in density of each scene, it became necessary to devise some means to alter the intensity of light the instant the scene changed.

By recording degrees of light intensity at given positions this was first accomplished, and afterwards by the rheostat. When the next scene was approaching the aperture, a notch in the side of the negative warned the operator and the light should be changed to meet the requirements of the density of the negative.

Primitive as this method was, it was a decided improvement, it nevertheless required considerable skill on the part of the operator, and was at the same time a trying operation.

Another interesting feature has been the evolution of chemical equipment. The old drums on which the films were originally developed required much space and apparatus in order to handle the desired quantites. Uniformity of output was next to impossible, owing to the fact that the large shallow tanks offered a great area of the developer to the air, thereby causing rapid oxidation, and a consequently rapid change in power and quality.

In the beginning, the negatives were of a very poor quality; grainy, and full of chemical fog. This was, of course, because of primitive ignorance in the compounding of developers. The operators used only their tested formulas, calculating in proportion—the results being far from satisfactory. Economy is often a spur to discovery. So it was in the development of films, the old formulas requiring immense quantities of sodas in proportion to the necessary amount of reducer. Enforced economy led to surprising discoveries—so that in the present day it would shock the ordinary photographer if we suggested to him a reversal of the proportions of the quantities as he has been accustomed to them.

It is interesting to re-visit one of the old "laboratories" with someone who has advanced with the business, and take a peep into the dingy buildings where the work was formerly accomplished under such trying conditions—bad light, bad air, operators dragging around the tremendous appliances from tank to tank, and misusing the films in the process. Then, turn to the present day laboratory with its light racks for the development of films in place of the clumsy old drums. Here a thousand or more feet of films can be developed at once, in tanks, thus insuring satisfaction in density and quality, and better uniformity. All this in rooms, clean, light and well-ventilated, on a square footage equal to one-fifth the capacity under the old methods.

Besides, there are the splendid, silently running printing machines, with their automatic light changes, of 15,000 feet capacity per day. These machines insure against scratches and other injuries, no part of their mechanism touches the films, and scratches are an impossibility. No matter what the atmospheric conditions may be or what the season, conditioned air service and thermostat systems insure perfect drying conditions.

The film manufacturer must not be forgotten in relation to the moving picture laboratory. So imperative has been the demand for cleanliness that there has been a gradual increase in the quality of raw film. It is amazing, but the picture is magnified to such an extent that a slight pin point imperfection assumes the proportions of a large aperture on the screen.

The manufacturers of chemicals have kept pace with our demand, also. An unprecedented standard of purity has been maintained, commensurate with the enormous amounts of sodas, etc., consumed in film production. The expert of

Drying Drums in Goldwyn Laboratory

Assembling Room—Ince Laboratories

Lewis W Physioc

Perforating Machines—Ince Laboratories

Washing the Film—Goldwyn Laboratories

the laboratory need make no chemical analysis of these products, for he knows their action so well that he can tell in an instant if they conform to the standard.

Did you know that one fixing bath requires 2,400 pounds of Hyposulphite of soda? Or would you believe that from $200 to $600 worth of silver is reclaimed from one bath of exhausted Hypo? Or do you have any idea of the cost of chemicals in a developing bath of 250 gallons? Do you know what the results on the screen would be if any of these chemicals were not quite up to their standard of purity?

Were we to attempt to read the riddle of the future of the motion picture by wandering through the vistas of the past, we would find ourselves in as much of a maze, technically, as in trying to adapt the ordinary photographic formulæ to the development of thousands of feet of modern motion picture negative.

What adds to our trepidation in predicting the future is the arrival of that latest innovation, the developing machine, whereby, automatically, thousands of feet are put through, carefully shielded from dust, without the touch of human hands, and the consequent dangers of handling while wet.

It seems pertinent to assume that within a very short time, the technicalities of film making will have become so perfected, that, like great books, music, statuary, and paintings, there will be incorporated in our fireside entertainment the motion picture home library.

It is a long, long way from the film box of the motion picture camera to the screen. All the work of every person identified with the making of the picture from the star to the lowliest scene shifter is in the balance until the superintendent of the laboratory announces what the results are. Only the most skilled workers are sought for employment in the laboratory. It is often within the province of the laboratory worker to "reclaim" some poor bit of work from the cameraman, often unavoidable, of course, because of conditions over which he sometimes has no control. If you are possessed of real ability to bring the best out of the negative in its transformation to the positive there is a chance for you to break into the movies—through the laboratory!

THE FILM EDITOR: HIS TRAINING AND QUALIFICATIONS

By DEL ANDREWS

For Many Years Film Editor, Thomas H. Ince Studios.

Editor's Note: Twelve years of active work in the motion picture industry is back of what Mr. Andrews tells you about Film Editing. Here is a man who has held practically every position of importance in a motion picture studio. Spending three years in the laboratory, he graduated to the rank of cameraman, where he devoted a year to that branch of the industry. Then came eighteen months as an assistant director, followed by a period in the literary department. Now, fulfilling the promise that Mr. Andrews made when he first came to the Ince Studios over five years ago, it is announced that he has been made a full-fledged director and placed in charge of a producing unit. Who is better qualified to tell you of one of the branches of the art which claimed his attention for a considerable period of time?

WHEN the camera ceases to record the final scene, when the megaphone is silenced, and the studio lamps switch their brilliant rays on to fresh scenes and faces, the hour of the film editor approaches. The thousands of feet of celluloid upon which are recorded the scenes of the photoplay but recently finished by the director, player and cameraman, are passed to the film editor. Then it is that he turns his attention to blending and grafting the new-born picture into a healthy, smooth-running story.

Few people appreciate the importance of the film editor's position. When it is realized that the success of a motion picture production is at stake in the cutting room, one will best be able to appreciate the great task that falls upon the man or woman who edits the film. The very best work of director or star can be ruined in the cutting room.

First, it would be well to point out the fact that in the making of a motion picture as many as fifty thousand feet of film are used, even though the finished picture seldom goes over seven thousand feet.

The director feels that in order to be certain that the picture will be properly photographed, as well as to be sure that the action will be consistent with the script, it is necessary to photograph each scene at least twice. Then, there are certain big sets that are photographed from many angles in search of one that will set the scene off to the very best advantage.

It is in the cutting room that every scene must be gone over with a view to trimming the unnecessary action. If the picture is padded or not properly cut, the audience will become bored and the reputation of the producing company, as well as the star, will suffer. At the time of filming the picture much of the action may have been deemed necessary to the director, only to be found superfluous to the proper presentation of the story on the screen. It is in the cutting room, however, that the actual worth of many of the scenes filmed is determined.

Therefore, it will be seen that the scissors play a large part in motion picture making. But not all of the film cut out of a picture is necessarily wasted. There are "cutters," as the film editor is sometimes called, that are so capable in their work that they are able to re-edit the cutouts of some pictures into brand new and sometimes really interesting pictures.

One excellent method of editing film, which has been adopted in many big studios, is to give the girl assemblers a layout which they follow, cementing the various strips in their proper order with the titles represented merely by numbers corresponding with numbers thrown on the screen. This gives the director an opportunity to view his own work, likewise giving him the opportunity of making whatever changes he deems necessary and adding any suggestions calculated to improve the titles before they are set up and photographed.

Where the studio employs a number of directors usually all of them sit in on the "pre-views" that are given a film before it is actually ready for the final release. They give freely of their thoughts and suggestions, and very often the years they have spent in their work is evidenced in the results achieved. Once approved, the master film is then made, and it is for this work that the many girl assistants in this branch of work are employed.

There can be no doubt about the fact that the assembling and cutting rooms offer many girls remunerative and interesting work. This is really one way of "Breaking into the movies." Once inside the studio as a worker in any capacity, there is no telling what the result may be if you are really qualified to do other and more important work.

To be qualified to become a film editor, one must have the ability to visualize the picture as it will look when screened. The cutting room is the place from which the picture graduates. To cut and edit a film play successfully, it is necessary for the executive in charge of that work to be "public-wise." The value of every scene and sequence must be carefully weighed and the man who attempts to do this must most surely be able to prepare and smooth the production for audience consumption.

Who is qualified to do this? Who is it that can condense fifty thousand feet of film to a solid concentrate of punch, action, and human interest? From my point of view I should say that anyone with the power to visualize a story in pictured form and with the knowledge of the pulse of the people, or should I say, one who can understand to the minutest detail, the effect of dramatic or comedy action upon that body of people which forms an audience; one who knows what will hold the interest of the public is possibly the person best fitted to undertake the cutting and editing of a motion picture production.

This field is not overcrowded. There are not any too many "good" film cutters or editors. There is opportunity in this branch of the movies and what is more to the point, great opportunity. But, the important question is are *you* fit for the work?

To be a good film cutter it is necessary to understand story construction; thoroughly, that is, to know what constitutes suspense, parallel action, dramatic values of each scene and sequence in both comedy and drama. For instance, a scene or sequence may have more value and may have a better hold on the audience if transposed and put into another place in the film proper. Would you know how to handle such a problem, to judge whether a certain scene would have greater dramatic value in one place than in another? Values in the motion picture story are often lost because the film editor allows a scene to run a fraction of a second too long or, conversely, does not allow it to run long enough.

To cut and edit film is a difficult matter, and my advice to those who are desirous of taking up this branch of movie work, is that they should first endeavor to secure a position in the cutting room in a menial capacity, and allow the best of all teachers to teach them the game. Who is the best teacher? Why, EXPERIENCE, of course!

DESIGNING CLOTHES FOR MOVIE FOLK

Information Concerning This Little-Known
Department

By EDITH CLARK

Costume Designer for Christie Film Company, Hollywood, California

THERE is probably no branch of cinemacraft more important than that allotted to the custodian of its sartorial effects. Her task is to see that the players are, at all times, faultlessly and beautifully attired. Not only for the purpose of emphasizing their good qualities but, also, in order to create the most logical interpretation of the character.

It would be difficult to imagine a woman in this position with a dour, cross-grained, easily ruffled temperament. Though she must be, in the truest sense of the word, a woman of genius, she is not in a position to be granted the right to display any of the eccentricities of genius. That qualification is limited to those with whom she comes in contact. If you are possessed of any of the foibles that are of an intensely irritating nature—then, indeed, abandon all hope of entering here.

Have you ever seen the fond mother of a half dozen kiddies planning a season's party frocks? Do you know that in the range of one family come wedding frocks, confirmation frocks, graduation frocks, masquerade and harlequin disguise, school frocks, and do you know that one brain usually plans the color schemes, the mending, the pressing, the turning, fitting and combining in the average home?

That mother is the head of the wardrobe department of a small institution, and her duties may be compared with the duties of one such woman in a great hive of industry, such as a moving picture studio.

She must co-operate in every detail with the work of the director, the producer, the star, and the author of the story. She must know perfectly the art of blending various fabrics, their colors and shades and the combinations of colors that get the best screen effects. Equipped with this knowledge, she must be alert, a first aid in emergencies and a mediator between the dressed and the dresser.

It is one thing to keep step with prevailing modes, planning costumes for plays of modern setting—but when it comes to historic films, rummaging through the chests of kings and princesses in the attics of antiquity, the paraphernalia is a far more complex matter.

To be authority on a camisole, petticoat and frock is one thing. To keep calculations on the shawl—pelisse—cape—mantilla — wrapper — plaid — kirtle — panier — apron — pinafore—girdle—is quite another story.

Shakespeare might well have been looking into the future on a motion picture screen when he declared that "the soul of this man is in his clothes." For, indeed, the soul of the film play is its proper costuming. A *faux pas* in connection with the dress of even the most inconspicuous member of the cast would create havoc with the entire production. That is to say, if one such blunder got out of the studio unnoticed.

To be a successful costumer, one must love clothes. Love designing as does the little girl dressing her dolls in the nursery, or parading before the mirror in grown-up clothes. One child begs auntie, mother or grandmother to make her dollies' dresses. Another begs for silks and laces and ribbons to make them herself and such a one would by no means permit another to fashion the fantastic creations for her adorable children. In the latter class is the embryo designer of motion picture costumes. It is that penchant, cultivated to the highest degree of artistic possibility, which gives to the motion picture industry the successful designer. There is no more delightful work.

The regrettable feature is that the audiences can never half conceive of the beauty of these creations, because the screen cannot portray the marvelously beautiful blending of color in wardrobe production. For, although the ultimate effect is only in the black, white and grey of the screen, color is a prime essential in the technique of photography. The richness of material combined with the brilliance of

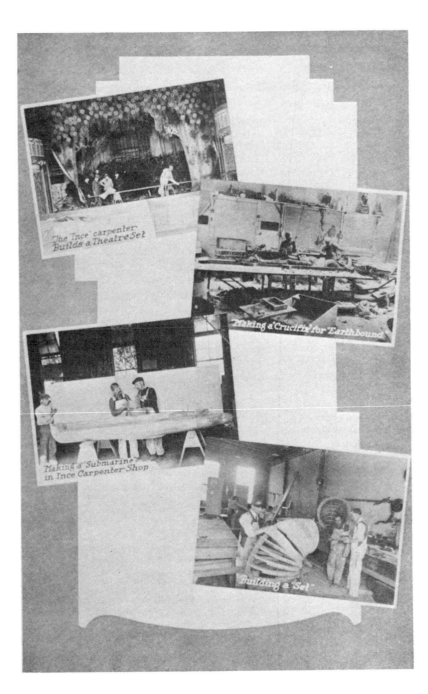

The Ince carpenter
Builds a Theatre Set

Making a Crucifix for Earthbound

Making a Submarine
in Ince Carpenter Shop

Building a "Set"

shade in fabrics gives a spectacular charm to the movie wardrobe that outrivals even an Oriental Bazaar.

As in so many branches of the industry, growth and progress have made such increasing demands upon the designer, that a new art has been born within the precincts of the studio. And film-costume designing stands alone unique in the march of artistic progress. Time was when the stage was the ne plus ultra of the designer's ambition. But this newer triumph of the silent drama, involving the knowledge of dress in every period of time—and intimate acquaintance with modeling, sketching, and painting, as well as other kindred arts, has indeed opened up new vistas to the costume creator.

One of the problems to be met in the designing of movie clothes is to get away from the date stamp—to lead the procession of style rather than follow in its train; to not contradict Dame Fashion, but rather to inspire her with new and lofty ideals. For how many women, today, are already copying the dresses of favorite screen stars, rather than consulting their style books or modistes.

It is a field of romance, adventure, and thrills, this costuming of screen folk for the world's inspection. But to attain anything like a triumph, to experience the thrill of satisfaction, one must be willing to travel the road, which, like all roads to success, is beset with difficulties, drawbacks and disappointments.

If you have patience, faith in your ability to think independently of the taste of a critical public—all the while acknowledging that eventually you must conform more or less to the caprices of that public and gratify its whims, if you are not afraid to work, work, work, and still do some more work, if clothes and their designing are a sort of holy fetish with you—then you have the right to assume that it would be worth your while to begin studying those things that will lead to the work of a designer.

If you have served your apprenticeship, and know your possibilities as well as your limitations, then indeed there is an opportunity for you in the wardrobe department of the studio. For after all is said and done, whether you must make a costume of peacock feathers, pearls and mirrors, or a plain little gingham sunbonnet, technique is the simple art of "knowing how."

There is sufficient variety to give wondrous zest to inspiration. One day you are designing a fluffy, gauzy, chiffon dance frock for a blonde beauty, and the next day you are showing up the grace of a rare brunette by draping velvets and silks which display her to the best advantage. And again you are conjuring with the tricks that turn the most winsome girl into a dangerously cunning vamp. The charm and mystery of plot construction in the brain of the author, offers no greater outlet for genius than does the designing of costumes that will carry out his interpretation of character through costumes.

The subtleties of silk, and lace, and fur, the witchery of shawl, and drapery, and frill, have been powerful forces in the world's history, and in more than a facetious sense, to this influence can be traced many a call "to arms."

If you are prepared to answer the age-old question "What shall I wear?" there is every chance for you to break into the movies through the Wardrobe Door.

THE PROPERTY MAN

Who Is Qualified to Become One?

By RAY CHRYSLER,

Master of Properties, Metro Pictures Corporation

PICTURE a curiosity shop and you can visualize clearly the property room of a large studio. In it, one will find everything from a suit of armor to a canary bird's nest. From it, several well-furnished homes or hotels could be outfitted. Complete with such appointments as fine linens and such accessories as art objects.

The term "prop" really covers everything. Sometimes it means a stable, another time a bull dog, a box of candy or an automobile, a work of art, of any of a million other things. In a motion picture studio, a "prop" means some object that is used in the making of the picture.

To qualify for fitness in being master of all this vast domain of materials, one must indeed have special training. The property man must be a very resourceful person, for it is up to him to know the location of any one of a thousand articles in his property room, and to be able to place his hand on almost anything that a director could call for in the work of filming a motion picture.

The property man has not as yet received his place in that limelight which seems to bathe all other studio executives. But when it is considered that a property man should have brains, initiative, and a good, retentive memory, it seems that he, too, is entitled to his share of glory. One thing is certain; he has a thousand times more worry and responsibility than his brother property man in the legitimate theatrical world.

It is from the ranks of the stage property men that many of the screen's property men are recruited. Still there are amateurs as well who have essayed the role of property man and have made good. To become a successful property man one must believe nothing impossible. Should he receive an order to produce a set of furniture of the time of the discovery of America, he must know or find out just what style of furniture was popular in those days.

Once he ascertains just what would be proper, he attempts to locate it and if it is not to be found, he must produce it. So he prepares plans, and then turns them over to the studio carpenter shop, where the needed articles or pieces of furniture are manufactured.

On an average, the property man has about twenty-four hours' notice of the various "props" that will be needed in a new production. Within that time two or two hundred pieces of furniture, a piano, a phonograph, a harp, a violin, twenty sets of curtains, half dozen rugs of various sizes or anything else imaginable must be in its proper place on the "set" where it is to be used. It is the duty of the Property Department to furnish all interior decorations that are not permanently attached to the walls of the settings themselves.

To care for this conglomerate assemblage of things, there is a department head and a corps of prop boys. Every article that goes out of the prop room is checked—the name of the picture in which it is to be used, the number of the stage which it is to be set on, and the number of scenes in which it is to be photographed. This is done for two reasons: first, to keep track of the articles; and second, it is a distinctive object, so that it wll not be used conspicuously in another picture. You see it would be very poor business if a handsome hand-carved chest, which adorned a star's New York apartment in one picture, were to be used in his Spanish castle in his next. People would say, "Well, they take their furniture right along with them, don't they?"

Many times articles of great value are used in pictures. These are sometimes rented from antique shops, or private collections. While they are in the studio they are in the care of the "prop" department, and checked out each day along with the rest of the studio props.

To illustrate the variety of props purchased or rented I might mention that Goldwyn recently rented a "freak" prop—a trained mocking bird for which they paid $5.00 a day (the wage of an extra man or woman).

THE LOCATION MAN: WHAT YOU MUST KNOW
TO BECOME ONE

By LOU STROHM

Location Manager, Metro Pictures Corporation

WITH the great advance that the motion picture business has experienced in the last few years, great changes have, of course, taken place in the personnel of the studio staffs maintained by the larger producing companies.

Of real importance to the smooth working of the producing unit is the location man. In the early days, the director did nearly everything in connection with the picture that he was directing—from painting some of the scenery to turning the crank of the camera, and finding the outside locations that his company was to use in the filming of exterior scenes.

Now, however, with the advance that has been made in the industry, each component factor of a picture is placed in the hands of one competent person, who presides over a particular department.

The location man, then, assumes a measure of importance in the daily scheme of the studio. What are his duties, and who can make good as a location man?

One of the first requisites of a location man is that he should know the surrounding country. A studio is situated in a given part of the country, but the script often calls for the filming of scenes that purport to represent an entirely different locality. It may, for that matter, involve another side of the world. Do you think it is necessary for the producer to go to the enormous expense of transporting the entire cast to the country or location the script calls for? On the contrary, the director merely notifies the location man that within a few days it will be necessary for the company to work in a street in Pekin, a high road in Brittany or among the Norwegian fjords. It is then up to the location man to find a suitable location.

How is this done? The location man knows the territory in the immediate vicinity of the studio where he is employed. In this way he eliminates the necessity of moving the company too great a distance in search of a certain location, when that location might be in close proximity to the studio. Out here in the rugged California country, it is usually not a difficult thing to find any required location.

By that, I do not mean to convey the idea that should the director call for a Spanish setting, the location man would be able to find a location built up to resemble a Spanish village or city. But, there are, in California, locations that because of their peculiar topography, are admirably adapted to the filming of scenes depicting far-distant places and·lands. Carpenters and scene makers build sets out in the open location and bring to the place the appearance of the native soil or surroundings that are to be depicted.

In bygone days the director was wont to ride about in a fast automobile seeking his own locations. This necessitated the spending of much valuable time.

Today, whenever the location man is on tour, and he comes across a spot that appears to hold valuable possibilities for future location for a given purpose, it is immediately photographed. Or, if there is no "still" camera available, the spot is carefully noted, and photographed at some future time.

Modern methods of motion picture producing demand that locations all be kept in elaborate index files, so that the moment the director advises the location man that he desires to film a certain scene, all the location man has to do is to refer to his files and bring forth pictures of a number of locations which are possibly suited to the needs of the story. In this way a great deal of time is saved and the director knows, before he reaches the scene, just what the place looks like.

For this reason, it is also well for the location man to understand the taking of "still" photographs.

Or sometimes the files, kept so religiously by his secretary, may not boast a photograph—though they may carry a very good description of the suitable location. It can be plainly seen, therefore, that the location man must also be able to dictate an authentic description of locations of which he has no photograph.

It would appear to me that the person best qualified to become a location man serving in California studios, is one who has spent a number of years in this state and surrounding states. It is all very well for a potential location man to know that Banff Springs, situated in middle westl ern Canada, is surrounded by wonderful mountain scenery adapted to the making of mountain scenes for a pic-turing of these requirements. But do you imagine a company would care to send its players to that distant location when a similar one might be found in the closely lying Sierra Nevada mountains? Yet both locations offer identical possibilities.

There are not many location men. It is not a field that is overcrowded, since each studio or producing company requires but one. As to the opportunity to break into the movie game as location man, there is this much to say. With the requirements I have mentioned, the possibilities for extremely important and highly interesting work are unlimited in this branch of the movies. Possibly you are particularly fitted to make a good location man. If so, why not make written application to one of the studios?

One of the Goldwyn Property Rooms

Section of Universal Property Room

Ray Chrysler

Dusting Goldwyn Bric-a-brac

Issuing Wardrobe to Extras

OPERATING THE PROJECTION MACHINE—PRACTICAL ADVICE FOR THEATRES, CHURCHES, SCHOOLS AND CLUBS

By EARL HAMILTON

Chief Projectionist, Grauman's Million Dollar Theatre

A FTER all is said and done, and the motion picture has made its way down from the very first shot to the softly-purring, electrically-run modern day projection machine, who is it that finally serves the public with its motion picture "food"?

Of great importance in the final steps of offering the picture to the public, is the man behind the motion picture "gun." The projecting machine is the "gun," and the projectionist is the man.

In a motion picture performance the operator of the projecting machine represents the whole company. He, with his machine, is in' the final link in the process of introducing the picture to the public. From this it can readily be seen that unless he is qualified to discharge his duties creditably, he can so tax the patience of the audience that the best film play in the world can be ruined. Upon him rests the success of a photoplay. Faulty projection has been the cause of more than one audience leaving a motion picture theatre in disgust, even though a great public favorite was occupying the screen.

The ranks of motion picture projectionists today are filled with serious-minded and conscientious workers. These men are qualified to handle properly thousands of dollars' worth of film that passes through their hands each working week. No longer can any boy secure a position as an operator, as projectionists were called in the earlier days of the film business. Today the theatre owner realizes that a great measure of his success depends upon the manner in which his pictures are screened. So we find motion picture projecting attracting a highly intelligent class of men.

For the man with some knowledge of electricity and its application, probably the best chance of breaking into the motion picture game is through the projection room. Manufacturers of projection machines have kept pace with all the improvements in the other branches of the industry, so that today we find comparatively few hand-power machines being manufactured for professional use. All are motor driven, and where in the old days a motion picture theatre had but one machine, it is now quite often the case that the projection room of the modern theatre is installed with as many as three machines.

An apprenticeship in the projection room familiarizes one with all the little tricks of the trade. These cannot be learned except by experience. My advice to anyone who wishes to become a motion picture projectionist is to get a speaking acquaintance with electricity first, and read some of the very good books that have been published on the subject of motion picture projecting, and which are advertised by the motion picture trade journals. Then make application to the theatres for a position. Therein may be the possibility of an initiation.

Once started, it will be well to bear in mind the importance of the post occupied. To appreciate fully the meaning of the work is to realize the projectionist's responsibility. The measure of success that a picture will attain, in his theatre at least, is due to a great extent to the way in which he offers that picture to its patrons.

THE EXHIBITOR'S OPPORTUNITY

By SID GRAUMAN

Editor's Note: It is with pleasure that I offer this chapter for the perusal of those interested in exhibiting Motion Pictures. Sid Grauman is one of America's pioneer exhibitors. From a beginning made years ago, the present day finds Mr. Grauman owner and manager of the finest Motion Picture Theatres on the Pacific Coast.

OF ALL the multitude of ambitious and intelligent persons looking toward "Movies" as the goal of their aspirations and as an industry in which to expand their talents, few select as a coveted job that of the Exhibitor.

And yet, it is the most fascinating of all. It is not only the most fascinating, but the most difficult and hazardous branch of the industry. When I declare that the qualification for success as an exhibitor is a rarer gift than qualification for success as a player, exploiter or producer, I really mean it! In saying this, I realize that I risk the rebuke of the thoughtless or unkind, who will doubtless credit me with egotism and conceit.

The producer's problems in the construction of a picture are general, not local. They can be treated in broad, sweeping generalities; but, the problems of the exhibitor are local and particular. No producer of a picture expects for it, no matter how great he may believe it to be, an equal measure of success in every state, county, city or town. He feels that in a general way he has compassed his intentions; has made a good picture that, in its appeal, will command the interest of the vast majority. On that assumption he proceeds. But the exhibitor must know, not only what his town wants, but what his own particular clientele wants. He must feel the pulse of his audience even, when alone, he sits in the projection room, and attempts to pass on the availability of this or that production for his house.

He must know how a picture may be improved by the introduction of music, prologue and atmospheric sets. In other words, he must be a first aid to the producer in accomplishing for a product what its creator could not do.

The passing whims, the transient "massed emotions" of his fellow-townsmen, must be watched, studied and appraised; the psychology of politics and other mental and spiritual forces that enter into metropolitan life must be scrutinized and weighed in the balance from day to day. For if the exhibitor fails to keep abreast of his day, or goes a minute or two in advance, he will likely make blunders of such an expensive character that he may soon cease to be an exhibitor. The producer may make a mistake in suiting this house or that, but if his picture has merit, it will find an audience somewhere in every city and town. If the exhibitor makes a mistake, all he can do is to withdraw the feature, tacitly confess his blunder, and with his week already half gone, try to substitute a success under odds overwhelmingly against him.

The reader will not, I trust, misconstrue these casual comments and interpret them as complaints, or imagine that between the lines there is a hidden whine. I rejoice in the difficulties that beset the path of the exhibitor, for there is a zest in overcoming obstacles, and a real joy that makes success worth while. Difficulties defy computation, for I verily believe that the showman is yet to be found who "learned" showmanship. It must be born in one and nurtured with infant digestion. I take it as a fairly well established fact that the successful exhibitors of today, either in pictures or connected with the spoken drama, are men brought up in the business from earliest boyhood; men who began, when they wore knickerbockers, to establish contact with the amusement-seeking public. There may be exceptions to this rule, but in most instances it is the old story of the exception proving the rule, and when such exceptions are studied it will be found that lack of early training has been overcome by the presence of great natural gifts.

The question is often asked, is it possible for attractions to be secured by new exhibitors—men entering the business without the advantage of strong affiliations. The answer is an emphatic affirmative. The trick is to know them when you see them; to recognize the merit of submitted pictures and not make too many mistakes.

Assuming that you have aspirations to become an exhibitor, and assuming your financial ability to manage the property problems of location, or site, and building, I would say unquestionably, that available and effective pictures can be secured in the open market, even though, at the time of your entrance into the business, all the well-known lines of picture distribution may be already held by prospective competitors.

But, I repeat, the trick is to make the right selections. Exhibitors affiliated with the established releasing organizations have the advantage, in that they are sure of a certain supply of standard products from approved hands and experienced producers. If such supply be unavailable to the newcomer with his new theatre, he still can have access to pictures made by experts, and produced under admirable conditions, but his problem will be to pick the winners. An exhibitor possessed of an infallible judgment, who knows absolutely what his public craves as entertainment, will have no trouble at all, for he will always choose superlative successes. Such a man will become a millionaire almost before his wife has grown accustomed to signing checks. All of which is facetious reasoning, for there is no such person as an infallible exhibitor. The difference between the successful exhibitor and the failure is merely a matter of degree. Both make mistakes; the failure makes the most.

I believe the tide of popular taste is turning slightly in favor of the spoken word. The balance is swinging back towards a more generous attention on the part of the public to the actor on the stage. I do not regard that fact with alarm, but rather with satisfaction; for taste for the spoken word is a normal taste. A public in which it were extinct would be an abnormal public and, therefore, difficult to please. The wise exhibitor is the one who accepts the dictum of the public and doesn't argue; one who believes that the public has reached the years of its maturity and is entitled to vote its own ticket. Friends may be made with the public by expanding the proportions and effectiveness of the prologue acts and the "atmospheric" prologue, in the creation of which I may claim, without boasting, to have been a pioneer.

I shall pass on to a brief consideration of music as one of the exhibitor's problems. The world in which we live is full of color and teeming with sound. Our senses of

perception are assailed every instant of our waking moments
—even in our dreams—with conceptions of color and sound.
The world of motion pictures is as silent as the craters on
the moon and as colorless as pencil drawings on white paper.
The element of color is absent, and perhaps permanently
absent from picture presentation; but the element of sound
can be controlled by music. Music wakes into life the
silences of the picture plot; it covers up the weakness—or
better still, it converts those silences into an eloquence beyond the power of words to attempt. Every emotion of
which the human soul is capable is within the scope of the
musical composer. That's why symphonic orchestras have
sprung into existence in motion picture theatres, that is why
marvelous organs have been perfected and installed,
and that is why the masterpieces of the world's greatest
composers are being constantly drawn upon, to give sublim-
ity and illusion to the otherwise soundless manifestations of
screenland.

Thus we find that the exhibitor must be not only a
potential politician, diplomat and student of psychology, but
he must choose wisely in the land of music, and he must be
—shall I admit it?—the world's most reckless gambler.
Does he not stake a fortune on the wisdom of his choice on
that most intangible, capricious and uncertain guess—*What
the public wants?*

DISTRIBUTING PICTURES ON THE STATE RIGHTS BASIS

By IRVING M. LESSER

President, Western Pictures Exploitation Co., Los Angeles, Cal.

N EW words and phrases have been coined to meet the needs of this great industry, and old words have taken on different shades of meanings.

There is, for example, the word *distribution*. In correlation to the business of manufacturing motion pictures it has come to mean the Alpha and Omega, the beginning and the end, for no producer who does not receive a proportionate return on his investment can continue to operate unless his pictures receive adequate distribution.

Let us, for the moment, glance at the fundamentals, the A, B, C, so to speak, of the motion picture industry.

"A" produces a motion picture. He delivers it to "B" for distribution. "B," the distributor, markets the picture. "C" is the buyer.

It will be readily seen that B is the important link in the chain, the one that must bear the weight; and no chain is stronger than its weakest link.

It is an axiom of the entertainment world that a good picture will always make money. Yet this axiom is tricky. It lulls many producers into a false sense of security.

A *good picture* will make money, but efficiently distributed by experienced showmen, it will make *more* money.

The question naturally arises how with such big companies in the field, is there a possibility for an independent producer to supply theatres with pictures, and at a profit. This would appear even more intricate when it is stated that the larger corporations, in some instances own or control big theatres in various sections of the United States.

The answer is to be found in what is known as State Rights distribution, though the independent producer is not confined exclusively to this phase of marketing.

All over the country there are big and little theatres which book independent-made products. There are several reasons for this. Possibly the theatre is too small to allow for the payment of a large sum for the first showing of an expensive picture. Yet this theatre manager does not want to wait until the picture has had a week's showing in the bigger theatre in his city and then play it. This is what is known in the vernacular as a second-run. The manager would prefer to offer his audience fresh stock, so to speak. Therefore he turns to the independent market for pictures, worthy productions which have not cost a tremendous amount of money to manufacture, and which can be rented at a more reasonable figure. Again, an independent production of exceptional merit always has a chance of being booked in the larger theatres, which means big rentals. Herein lies the golden opportunity for the independent producer. He should strive for exceptional pictures.

Independent productions, must have *merit*. It is not necessary, though, that they be based on expensive stories and made by high-priced directors.

Too much care and consideration cannot be given to the story. It is the strength, the sinew of a picture. There are active and trustworthy firms and agents ready and willing to advise a producer on literary matters, and it will be found generally that their opinion regarding stories for the screen is commercially sound.

Once a story is selected the producer should by all means confer with a distributor to determine the exploitation possibilities of the completed picture. The Western Pictures Exploitation Company has found, at the time that this is being written, a keen demand for Western pictures. Yet between now and press time the market may change.

Because "The Miracle Man" was a tremendous success cannot be accepted as proof positive that the American theatre-going public will always patronize a miracle picture. Indeed, I cannot call to mind any one of the numerous "miracle" pictures which followed "The Miracle Man" that made any great amount of money. This, in itself, proves the value of a marketing or distributing organization in Los Angeles. The distributor can keep the producer advised on

Interior of Grauman's Million Dollar Theatre
Los Angeles Cal.

Sid Grauman

Detail
Grauman's Million Dollar Theatre

Usherette
Grauman's Million Dollar Theatre

market conditions. The American public is as fickle in its entertainment taste as it is in its fashions, and the distributor must be ever alert to keep abreast of the times and know what the public wants.

Heretofore the business of distributing, which means the marketing of pictures, has been carried on almost exclusively from New York.

To my mind, there existed a gap between producers and the market which should have been bridged. New York was too far from Los Angeles. There seemed no logical reason why films should not be distributed from Los Angeles. There appeared to me to be many convincing reasons why there should be a distributing center here, not the least of which was the fact that the manufacturer would be in close touch with the man who was selling his product.

This was not merely a theory on my part. I had been associated with Sol Lesser in the marketing of "The Spoilers," "Hearts of the World," "Yankee Doodle in Berlin," "The Ne'er Do Well," "Civilization," "20,000 Leagues Under the Sea," "Intolerance," "The Garden of Allah," "Peck's Bad Boy," and numerous other big feature productions.

The business of producing and marketing pictures is so diversified that no producer to date has been able himself to combine both elements.

I don't think half the motion pictures released today are being worked to the maximum of their earning power.

Motion pictures have been and will always be the most romantic and profitable of all of America's vast industries. There is an element of hazard in every business, yet it is possible through wise selection of material, proper casting and direction, and efficient distribution to reduce motion picture making to a stable commercial basis. Therein lies the romance, however, for any picture is apt to develop into a gold mine. This one element has prompted numerous investors to follow that age-old adage of the miner, and to go it blind. There can be but one result in business for the man who sets out to make a product without being conversant with the market. It would not be a wise undertaking to make dress suits for the natives of Tahiti.

There is a staple market for good entertainment. The market does, however, as stated in the foregoing, change occasionally as regards a specific type of product.

While it has been my aim to make this article general in its various phases it might be well to tell just how a picture is handled on a state rights basis.

When a picture is completed it is subjected to a screen examination or "preview." Knowing the accurate status of the market the distributor sets an "exhibition value" on the production. That is to say he estimates that the picture is worth a specified sum for the entire United States. These figures are based on the public demand for this particular type of picture, and the knowledge that it would be played by an aggregate number of big and little houses to return the exhibition value.

Maps in the offices of distributors divide the United States into areas. For example, a San Francisco film exchange controls Northern California, Nevada and the Hawaiian Islands. A Los Angeles film exchange controls the territory embracing Southern California and Arizona. And so on elsewhere in the United States.

Territorial rights are then disposed of to the various exchanges. The negative of the production remains in a Los Angeles laboratory, prints being made here and expressed C. O. D. to the film exchanges.

The distributor, meanwhile, has made up attractive booklets and sheets with suitable publicity matter, selected interesting "still" photographs of scenes of the play, and has had lithographs made for lobby and other outdoor display.

This is the procedure for a single production. Distributors also market various "series" of pictures. These pictures, in series, are sold in advance, contracts being made at one time for the entire series.

SCOPE AND OUTLOOK OF VISUAL EDUCATION

Editor's Note: To J. Paul Goode, Professor in Chicago University, goes the credit for this very interesting paper on the Scope and Outlook of Visual Education. Mr. Goode has had the opportunity to determine the value of visual education in his University classrooms and sets down herewith his views on the subject which are given through the courtesy of the Society for Visual Education's magazine, "Visual Education."

IT IS hardly necessary to remind ourselves of the fact that the psychologists have always been telling us that of all the senses, sight leads as an avenue of sense perception. Of that fact we are all of us sure. Nor is it news to most of us that sense perceptions are vastly reinforced and deepened when added avenues of sense are contributing to the presentation. We prove this to ourselves in a hundred ways every day. But it is one thing to state the fact and believe it and quite another thing to put it to use profitably in our formal education. Traditions in education, like other habits, persist, perpetuate themselves and may be hard to displace when better methods come along. We have grown so accustomed to the printed page as the foundation of school education—so satisfied with the old routine of assigning so much text and demanding a reaction from the pupil in some oral or written test, that it may be actually something of a shock to have a change suggested. Yet when we take an account of stock we discover that the printed page is one of the slowest means of presenting a wide range of information. To see a coral reef for even a few minutes will give a far more vivid and intimate realization of its character than any amount of printed description could do. With the impressions of the reef seen, felt, heard and smelt, a foundation is laid for a life-long interest in all sorts of printed or spoken description and discussion of coral reefs.

But the world is large, and most people are rooted to the daily task. They cannot pick up and go to the ends of the earth to see the many things it is well to know about. So to the aid of the printed page has been brought more and more, in recent years, many devices in visual education to enlist the eye in arousing interest, deepening impressions, making it easier and quicker for the student to learn and to retain the lesson.

It is my purpose in this paper to make a survey of the various ways, beyond the printed page, in which the eye may be utilized profitably in the business of education. And then to make a plea for the correlation of the different agencies and the best application of them in educational practice.

One of the oldest studies in the school—Geography— was the first to take advantage of visual methods. The map is a system of shorthand in the presentation to the eye of space relations. From the earliest time it presented areas in two dimensions and came later, by one pictorial device or another, to suggest land relief, the third dimension. The map has always been a part of the fundamental equipment in geographic instruction. And yet it has never been made to give its best service to the pupil. In all geography rooms globes and maps are essential, but the very great value of the desk outline map to be filled in by the pupil, in exercises and tests on distribution, is an open and largely untilled field in education. For we are not only eye-minded, we are hand- or motor-minded; and working on a map has possibilities in education largely overlooked.

And because we are motor-minded and because it is a good investment in education to enlist other senses than that of sight, the museum has been developed. Every museum is an investment in popular education, the value of which now is generally conceded. And the museum has here and there been put to work in the interest of school education. Perhaps the best development in America has been achieved by the Philadelphia Commercial Museum. As an aid in the teaching of geography, but especially of Commercial Geography, this museum has prepared many traveling collections with sets of articles, which are sent gratis to the schools, to be used for a specific time in classroom instruction. The exhibits are made up of samples of various commodities of commerce, such as textiles, raw and manufactured, cabinet woods, grains, ores, metals and other materials, which have in them a little bit of the reality of the world about which the pupil is reading and studying.

Very early also the geographer introduced the picture as an aid in the presentation of his subject. But it is only in recent decades that the value of the picture has been demonstrated in many other lines as well as geography. A reading book in the lower grades nowadays is unthinkable without generous illustration. All the sciences and arts use the picture and the diagram in increasing measure in texts and in articles for general reading. Botany, zoology, anthropology and geography would be crippled beyond measure without the prolific picture. The growing generosity of illustration by the current magazine and certain daily papers has been a godsend to the schools wherever live teachers have undertaken to collect and use these pictures as an aid in classroom instruction. One of the best services rendered by any periodical in this country has been that of the lavishly illustrated *National Geographic Magazine*. Its collection of pictures now runs to over fifty thousand and they are being reprinted and made available at cost for individual pupil's use.

The success of this picture phase of visual education has been marked. But it has required some genius to get best results. The pictures are as a rule too small for class use. They may be studied individually, but it is difficult to get a class discussion without having a picture large enough for use before the class entire. This early led to the use of projection lantern.

But the lantern of early days was a cumbersome thing. It called for a darkened room, which has been always somewhat difficult to manage. Then the illuminant was a messy affair, with tanks of oxygen and hydrogen and candles of lime, always slacking into dust; the whole outfit dangerous in the hands of a novice and requiring a skillful operator. Thus the lantern could be used only by the school entire and largely for entertainment, not instruction. The coming of electricity gave much more freedom, but even here the danger of open circuits, and the attention to the open arc, have kept the equipment out of common use.

The coming of the Mazda filament lamp, however, has thrown all barriers down. Now little projection lanterns are available at small cost, and every school building may have one or more such lanterns. The lantern is coupled into any lamp socket, it can be safely managed by any child, the light is so intense that the darkening of the room is not a serious matter. The lantern now may be ready for service at a minute's notice in any room where the electric current is available. And by means of the reflectoscope, book and magazine illustrations become available, also.

The lantern makes possible and profitable the use of many maps and graphs as well as pictures. Here is a very large avenue of service, which is little developed. A map can be copied into a lantern slide and colored for a dollar or so and thrown on the screen on a scale much larger than any printed map obtainable. This gives unlimited freedom to the instructor for many maps which we may never hope to have published in large form, could be used with profit in the class room. To make one such map would require much time and skill, and might cost fifteen or twenty dollars or more. Then, too, a hundred and fifty such maps in the form of lantern slides can be stored in one drawer of the ordinary card catalog cabinet of the library, whereas in the ordinary printed form, in rolls and on sticks, a whole room would be required for storage.

The graph is a device in visual education which has large possibilities and is but little developed. A whole page of statistics can be thrown into the form of a curve, as for example, the production of wheat year by year for a generation, and the trend of production can be read at a glance. Wheat export for the same years can be thrown into another curve and the two curves compared. The price of wheat can also be entered, and such combinations offer the finest opportunities for discussion and interpretation. I have seen great audiences of the best educated men and women sitting on the front edge of their chairs, in rapt attention, as some interpretation has been read from maps and graphic statistics. One may notice the conspicuous success of the Babson curves of business expansion and depression, and the growing use of graphics in many lines of business, to realize something of the possibilities of this form of visual education.

The photograph, the print, the lantern slide have done splendid service in the school room, but the finest service yet rendered has been done by the stereograph. The photograph presents but two dimensions. At best it suggests the third dimension. We are generous and supply out of our own experience the third dimension. But the stereocamera and the sterescope work a miracle. They supply the actuality of binocular vision, and the third dimension is presented to the eye in vivid reality. This is a degree of perfection the camera alone can never give. The person who looks through th stereoscope looks upon the real mountain, looks into the depths of the real canyon, looks upon the actual statue, the actual cathedral.

The stereoscope a generation ago was an interesting and entertaining novelty, little more. Its place was on the parlor table, along with the reading lamp and the family Bible. But it has won its spurs now as one of the best devices in visual education yet developed. For the stereoscope, with its charm of intense reality, comes to have a teaching power 'of the highest value. But like many another teaching device, it was tried in the schools and failed to hold its own until long study and analysis of its possibilities in actual use had determined the correct mode of employing the stereoscope.

By going into the school room and earnestly watching the boys and girls react under the stimulus of this marvelous instrument, it was learned how it could be made best to serve the purpose of school room work. It was discovered that the stereograph must be worked, but not overworked. It must help get the day's lesson, not get in the way of the lesson. It must occupy the student without the attention of the eacher. I must lead the pupil to apply himself and learn for the pleasure of learning.

The method is simple. An ample supply of stereographs is provided. The number in one standard set runs to 600. The subjects are chosen to cover the whole earth, and with selections so made as to cover many topics which will be studied in geography, in history, in literature. These stereographs are classified into all the topics where their use may be profitable, cross-referenced and indexed, and the whole study published in book form, as a Teacher's Guide, so that the teacher may find any stereograph available for teaching any subject as easily as she can find a word in the dictionary, and can put her hand right on the required stereograph without a moment's delay.

Each stereograph has on the reverse side a description running to 250 words, written in an interesting style and carrying the necessary information to the student. In use the teacher puts out the stereoscope and one or two stereographs, relating to the next day's lesson. Sometime during the study periods of the day each pupil will study the stereograph, read the description and be ready next day to tell what he saw. It becomes a game to see who can stand and report in good English what he saw looking through the window of the stereoscope into the reality beyond. At the end of the week, or when the review on the country or topic comes, the same views, in lantern slide form, are put before the whole class, and some pupil is chosen to stand before the class and discuss what one view presents and other pupils report on other slides.

A real interest is aroused. Better teaching results. Live material is in hand always for drill in geography, history, English. The success of the method is unquestioned. The sets of views are in use in thousands of schools all over the country. It is the best contribution yet made in visual education in America.

The stereograph arrives at perfection in presenting the perception of solidity and distance, the third dimension of the view. There is nothing to compare with it in this service, but it is a static world. The waterfall is a frozen waterfall. The wave is an arrested wave. Motion is absent. Yet motion is another "dimension" and the presentation of motion in the picture is an arrival at another apex of perfection. The jetting, plunging water of the cataract is there, before the eyes. The gracefully moving animal, the rushing waves, the swaying trees, are all there, to the last perfect detail of motion. The marvel of it, this interest has been catered to by using the film as an amusement, because, of course, people are always ready to pay well for being amused. So compelling, so persistent, so universal is this interest in the film that, as we are now told, the cinema business is one of the largest three or four industries in the whole country.

Examining Negative in Process of Development

Women Laboratory Workers

Teaching Animal Actors to "Act"

Photographing the Cartoon

Projection Room
Grauman's Million Dollar Theatre

stood at 10 per cent. In the 5,000 childre
schools, between the kindergarten and the
cutting the failures from 10 per cent to 5 pe
promotion to 250 pupils, who without the improve
tion would have been ranked as failures and wou
been required to repeat the course. To have ha
pupils repeating the course would have called for six or \
extra teachers and extra rooms. On the basis of the avera,
cost of a year's schooling, this promotion of 250 pupils was
a saving to the taxpayers of Racine of between $10,000 and
$15,000 in the year. Think of what the saving to the whole
country will be, when visual education in all its phases has
been fully worked out and entered to the game in all the
schools!

There are in the common schools of the country at this
time, in the grades below the high schools, over 20,000,000
pupils enrolled. The record shows over 15,000,000 in
attendance. The average annual cost per pupil in these
schools in 1914 was not far from $30 each. This cost has
doubtless doubled since then. An average of ten per cent
failure in this number gives us 1,500,000 pupils to repeat the
work. This, at $60 per pupil, makes the very respectable
sum of $90,000,000 per year. Suppose now, the introduction
of visual education could cut this failure record down five
per cent on the average. That would make a neat sum of
$45,000,000 per year, a prize well worth working for. Now
not only can this improvement be made in the grades, it can
be made in some measure in the secondary schools as well.
The equipment thus made ready may serve in Americaniza-
tion work in churches and in community centers. This is a
wide and magnificent opportunity for service. It is worthy
the best brains and most serious effort of all of us.

A PREDICTION

ALEXANDER GRAHAM BELL, inventor of the telephone, is said to have once predicted that "some day in America 200,000 telephones will be in daily use."

In more than one city today there are alone greatly in excess of 200,000 telephonic connections. Yet Bell's auditors are declared to have viewed the prediction with smiling incredulity.

There are doubtless many educators in America at this time who will question the prophesy that within the next decade, visual education will be employed in practically every school and college in the United States; that subjects now taught with textbooks will be better taught with motion picture film; that many present-day methods of instruction will become obsolete—swept aside by the superiority of the projection machine.

Professor Goode's arguments in favor of visual education merely emphasize the indubitable fact that there *must* be a place in motion pictures for the educator.

Who is better qualified to direct the making of educational pictures than the educator himself?

Who is better equipped than the educator to write the scenarios necessary for the making of educational film?

Visual education is a new art; and to those pioneer teachers of today who have the vision to foresee the future of the educational picture, the rewards of a later day will probably be beyond their fondest dreams.—THE EDITOR.

Dictionary

A MOTION PICTURE DICTIONARY

DEFINITIONS OF WORDS AND PHRASES USED IN PICTURE MAKING

Reprinted by courtesy of the Educational Department,
Palmer Photoplay Corporation

NOAH WEBSTER compiled the first American dictionary—but since his time the coming of motion pictures has caused the coining of many new words. Here, then, is a Motion Picture Dictionary. First comes the:

ACTION: The connected series of events forming a photoplay; the unfolding of the story; the various actions of individual characters whereby the story is advanced.

ANGLE-SHOT: Another view of a continuous scene taken from a different telling of the story.

BRIEF SYNOPSIS: The synopsis of a scenario reduced to the briefest telling of the story.

BUSINESS: A definite bit of action. "Business of climbing a ladder" would indicate that a character referred to would climb a ladder at a point thus designated in a scenario.

BUST: An obsolete term for close-up.

CAMERA: The motion picture camera with which the picture is made. This camera must not be confused with the camera with which still pictures are made.

CAMERA MAN: The operator of the motion picture camera.

CAPTION: A synonym of sub-title, seldom used.

CAST: An abbreviation of *cast of characters.*

CAST OF CHARACTERS: An itemized list of the characters appearing in a photoplay.

CHARACTERS: The various fictitious persons who take part in a photoplay story.

CINEMATOGRAPHER: The expert photographer who operates a motion picture camera.

CLIMAX: The height of upward movement in the action; the supreme moment in a photoplay; the conclusive point toward which all the action has been directed.

CLOSE-UP: A scene or character photographed with the camera close to the action; a close view.

CONFLICT: A strife for mastery; hostile contest or encounter; competition or opposing action of incompatibles; antagonism as to divergent interest. Used in the same sense as struggle.

CONTINUITY: Name for a photoplay in its technical form. When a story is made for the director, it is put in continuity form. The scenes are set down in the sequence they are desired to appear on the screen. They need not, however, be photographed in this squence. Each scene, as it is photographed, is numbered with the number corresponding with that scene in the CONTINUITY BOOK. When all the scenes of the continuity have been photographed, they are assembled, in sequence from Scene No. 1 on down to the last scene.

CONTINUOUS ACTION: A scene taking place in a single location between the same characters, or in a series of locations in which the action of the characters is followed without interruption other than short cut-backs to break the scene. This requires skillful handling in order to sustain interest and keep the action confined to the central characters.

CRANK: A studio term meaning to photograph. (See shoot.)

CRANKING: A studio term for photographing, derived from the act of the cinematographer turning the camera crank.

CRANK-SPEED: Used to indicate the speed at which the picture should be photographed to regulate action.

CRISIS: A critical moment in the development of the story, not as important as the climax.

CUT-BACK: The return to a scene after showing interpolated scenes of related action.

CUTTING: A finished feature length film usually means about 6,000 feet of film. This is projected upon your theatre screen and makes the feature picture of the evening. But before this is shown, much cutting has taken place because the directors take as much as 50,000 feet of film to make up a picture of feature length. Therefore, the 50,000 feet must be *cut* down to approximately 6,000 feet.

DESCRIPTIVE-TITLE: A sub-title used to describe that which is not shown in action or to cover a lapse of time.

DIRECTOR: One who directs the production of a photoplay.

DISSOLVE: To dissolve, or blend, one scene into another.

DISCOVERED: A term used to designate that a character is already on a scene when it appears on the screen.

DOUBLE EXPOSURE: When a phantom or visionary effect is desired to blend two parts in one scene which cannot be photographed at one time, a double exposure is made. Often used to show the thoughts of a character.

DRAMATIC TRIAD: A union or group of three characters or groups of characters, closely related in the action of a photoplay.

DREAM PICTURE: A photoplay of an improbable nature finally explained as being a dream.

ENTER: A term used to designate the entrance of a character into a scene.

EPISODE: A section of a serial photoplay, usually consisting of two reels.

ESTABLISH: To make known the relationship of a character to other characters or to his environment, or to make known his identity and type.

EXIT: A term used to designate a character leaving a scene.

EXPLANATORY-TITLE: A sub-title used to explain that which is not made sufficiently clear in action.

EXTERIOR: A scene in which the action takes place out of doors.

EXTRAS: (Extra men and women.) Actors of minor parts who are engaged by the day. People employed for some special scene. Also known as atmosphere.

FACTION: A distinct character or set of characters acting in opposition to other characters or sets of characters; the three characters or sets of characters in a dramatic triad are known as "factions" in photoplay phraseology.

FADE-IN: A gradual appearance of a scene upon the screen.

FADE-OUT: A gradual disappearance of a scene upon the screen.

FAKING: Making the unreal appear real; mechanical or camera devices employed to produce results that appear to an audience startling and impossible.

FARCE: Comedy in which great latitude is allowed as to probability of happenings and naturalness of characters.

FILM: The strip of celluloid coated with photographic emulsion and used in motion picture photography.

FILMING: Producing; filming a play in studio vernacular for producing.

FLASH: The appearance of a scene or fragment of a scene on the screen for a brief moment.

FRAME: Each single picture on a film.

FREE LANCE: A writer who is free to submit his work generally and is not in the pay of any one company.

INSERT: Any still matter other than a sub-title inserted in a film, such as the reproduction of letters, newspapers, telegrams, bottle-labels, small objects, etc.

INTERIOR: A scene in which the action takes place indoors. (Most interiors are photographed in sets constructed on open-air stages.)

INTRODUCTORY-TITLE: A sub-title used to introduce a character.

IRIS: The adjustable diaphragm for regulating the aperture of a lens.

IRIS IN: To open the iris on a scene in order to enlarge from a tiny speck to full size.

IRIS OUT: To close the iris on a scene in order to reduce gradually from full size to a tiny speck.

LABORATORY: A department of a studio devoted to the process of developing negative, printing positive, etc.

LEAD: A leading character in a photoplay, either male or female.

LEADER: A sub-title. (This term is practically obsolete, sub-title having replaced it.)

LIGHTING: Generally used to designate tinting, as for moonlight effects, shadow effects or strong lights on a situation to be emphasized.

LIGHT STUDIO: An enclosed studio equipped with glass sides and roof or with artificial lighting systems for photographic purposes.

LOCALE: The locality, surroundings or environments in which a photoplay or a separate sequence of scenes is laid.

LOCATION: Any place outside a studio where a scene is photographed.

LOCATION LIST: An itemized list of locations to be used in the production of a photoplay, appended to a working script.

LONG-SHOT: A scene photographed with the camera at a distance from the action; a full view.

MAIN-TITLE: The name of the story as a whole.

MANUSCRIPT: A scenario in typewritten form, inclusive of all its various parts.

MAT: (Keyhole mat—binocular mat, etc.) A plate with an opening of a peculiar shape to fit over the lens. A keyhole, for instance, through which a scene is photographed to give the appearance of being viewed through a keyhole.

MENTAL "PUNCH": Dramatic value in thought.

MULTIPLE REEL OR MULTIREEL: A photoplay, consisting of more than one reel, but usually referring to a photoplay of greater length than five reels.

NEGATIVE: The raw film used in motion picture photography. After the negative has been exposed in the camera, it is developed and from this the positive is printed.

PAN OR PANORAM: A contraction of panorama or panoramic; moving the camera up and down, or from side to side to follow the action from one place to another.

PHOTODRAMATIST: One who creates photodramas.

PHOTOPLAY: A story told in pictured action instead of words.

PHYSICAL "PUNCH": Dramatic value in situations.

PLOT: The elaboration of an idea or theme, showing cause, effect and sequence. (See Theme.)

POSITIVE: The film printed from the negative and used in the projection of pictures. The same process is used that you would use to make prints from your Kodak negative.

PRINCIPALS: The actors or actresses who play the principal parts in a photoplay.

PRODUCER: One who produces pictures. The director is in charge of the actual direction of the action of a photoplay, while the producer usually supervises the work of one or more directors and frequently is the financial head of a company.

PROJECTING MACHINE: A machine used in motion picture theatres for projecting the picture to the screen.

PROJECTION: The act of throwing a motion picture on the screen. (See Screen.)

PROPS: An abbreviation of properties; the various articles or objects used in producing a photoplay.

PROP. LIST: An abbreviation of property plot.

PROPERTY PLOT: An itemized list of objects and articles used in the production of a photoplay.

READER: One employed to assist a scenario editor in reading submitted manuscripts.

REEL: The metal container upon which film is wound; the standard unit used in measuring photoplay films, aggregating one thousand feet.

REGISTER: To indicate or record. An actor registers "hatred" or other emotions in a scene.

RELEASE: Pictures are made and very often stored away until the producer is ready to "release" them.

RELEASE DATE: A previously arranged date upon which a photoplay is released for exhibition throughout the country.

RELEASE TITLE: The main-title finally chosen for a photoplay when it is completed and ready to be released.

RELIEF: A bit of comedy or light dramatic action interpolated in or following a heavy dramatic scene to relieve the dramatic tension.

RETAKE: Photographing a scene a second time on account of some defect in the first.

RETROSPECT: To revert to previous action. As for instance, a character is relating to a policeman the details of a robbery in which the character figured. The action is dissolved from the scene of the character talking to the policeman, to the scene of the robbery and then dissolved back to the character finishing his narrative. The scene of the robbery may or may not have been previously depicted.

SCENARIO: The outline of a photoplay, indicating the scenes and the entrances, action and exits of the actors, together with sub-titles and inserts.

SCENARIO EDITOR: A person employed by a producing company to read submitted manuscripts and select therefrom those suitable for production.

SCENE: The action in a photoplay that is taken without stopping the camera.

SCENE-PLOT: The itemized layout of scenes for the convenience and guidance of a director.

SCREEN: The plain surface on which a photoplay is projected.

SCRIPT: An abbreviation of manuscript.

SEMI-CLOSE-UP: A scene photographed with the camera a little further distant than in a close-up, but closer than a long-shot.

SEQUENCE: A connected or related succession of events; a connected series of incidents.

SETS: All interior locations are indicated as sets. (Scenery painted on canvas strips.)

SHOOT: A studio term meaning to photograph. (See Crank.)

SHOT: When a scene is photographed by a motion picture camera, it is known as a shot. A scene photographed from a distance is known as a LONG-SHOT. A large set must be taken from a distance to be certain that all of it will appear on the screen.

SILHOUETTE: A figure or figures shown dimly to heighten an effect.

SITUATION: A temporarily unpleasant, unfortunate, trying or involved relation of affairs at a moment of action; a predicament.

SLOW-CRANKING: Cranking the camera slower than usual speed in order that the action may be accelerated when the picture is projected at the regular speed. Frequently used in comedy chases, etc. Cranking eight, cranking twelve, etc., means to expose that number of frames per second instead of the usual sixteen frames per second, which is regulation speed. To slow this, operation is reversed.

SPECTACLE: A photoplay of a spectacular nature, such as "Intolerance."

SPLIT-REEL: A one thousand-foot reel containing more than one object. This usually refers to a five-hundred-foot story and is practically obsolete.

SPOKEN-TITLE: A sub-title used to interpret that which is spoken by a character in a photoplay.

STAFF-WRITER: A scenario writer engaged by a producing company at a regular salary.

STILL: A photograph made with an ordinary camera, showing a scene or characters from a photoplay, usually used for advertising purposes.

STRUGGLE: To put forth great efforts; to strive, to contend, as one character or faction strives against and contends with another.

STUDIO: A headquarters where photoplays are made.

STUNTS: Effects out of the ordinary, trick camera work, hazardous action in comedy or drama.

SUB-TITLE: A word, phrase or sentence appearing on the screen during the projection of a photoplay.

SUSPENSE: The quality of uncertainty, anxiety or expectation aroused by a sequence of scenes.

SWITCH-BACK: Same as cut-back.

SYNOPSIS: The general view of a story; an abstract or summary; narrative.

TECHNIQUE: The definitely established and skillful system of procedure by which an idea is expressed in proper form.

TELESCOPIC LENS: A lens used for telescopic or long distance photography.

THEME: The motive or subject; the thread of the story; the central idea. (See Plot.)

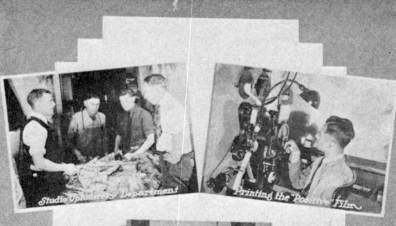

Studio Upholstery Department

Printing the "Positive" Film

Making the "Titles"

Negative Cutting Room—Universal Studios

The Wardrobe Department

THRILLS: Startling or intensely dramatic action; spectacular, frequently dangerous and often unexpected.

TIME ELAPSE: Accounting for the time intervening between scenes indicated by a sub-title or a fade-out or both.

TINTING: The process of chemically dyeing positive films to produce special effects, such as twilight, night, moonlight. (See Lighting.)

TRUCK-BACK: The act of moving the camera back from action as it is being photographed.

VIGNETTE: A close-up of an article or countenance generally used in lieu of a masked photograph.

VISION: A scene within a scene produced by double exposure and used to convey to the audience the thoughts of a character.

VISUALIZATION: The act or power of forming visual images or mental representations of objects not present to the sense.

WIDE-ANGLE LENS: A lens covering an angle wider than the ordinary. Lenses for ordinary purposes have an angle of 50 per cent or less. Wide-angle lenses may cover as much as 75 per cent, and are useful for photographing at short range.

WORKING SCRIPT: The scenario in tabloid form, including locations, general "business," entrances and exits and the mechanical evolution of the story.

WORKING TITLE: The main title used for purposes of convenience and record during the production of a photoplay. The working title is usually succeeded by a more carefully chosen main title after the photoplay is completed. (See Release Title.)

ABBREVIATIONS

EXTERIOR—Ext.

INTERIOR—Int.

BACKGROUND—B. G.

MIDDLEGOUND—M. G.

DISCOVERED—Disc.

PANORAMA—Pan.

MANUSCRIPT—Mss. or Script.

BUSINESS—Bus.

CLOSE-UP—C. U.

ENTER—Ent.

EXIT—Ex.

PROPERTIES—Props.

Directory
of the Leading Motion Picture Studios

AMBASSADOR PICTURES CORPORATION, 906 *Girard Street, Los Angeles, Cal.*
AMERICAN FILM COMPANY, *Santa Barbara, Cal.*
ART-O-GRAF FILM COMPANY, *Englewood, Denver, Col.*
ASTRA FILM CORPORATION, *Verdugo Road, Glendale, Cal.*
ATLAS EDUCATIONAL FILM COMPANY, 1111 *South Blvd., Oak Park, Chicago, Ill.*
ATLAS FILM CO. OF AMERICA, 705 *West 8th Street, Los Angeles, Cal.*
ARGUS ENTERPRISES, 815-823 *Prospect Ave., Cleveland, Ohio.*
ART ANIMA FILM STUDIO, 113 *Nineteenth Street, Rock Island, Ill.*
LEAH BAIRD PRODUCTIONS, *Ince Studio, Culver City, Cal.*
SNOWY BAKER PRODUCTIONS, 3800 *Mission Road, Hollywood, Cal.*
BALSHOFER PRODUCTIONS, INC., 1329 *Gordon Street, Los Angeles, Cal.*
F. J. BALSHOFER STUDIO, 1329 *Gordon Street, Los Angeles, Cal.*
REGINALD BARKER PRODUCTIONS, *Culver City, Cal.*
BEAR STATE FILM COMPANY, *Hollywood, Cal.*
BERWILLA FILM CORPORATION, 5821 *Santa Monica Blvd., Hollywood, Cal.*
BLANCHARD FILM COMPANY, 7870 *Santa Monica Blvd., Hollywood, Cal.*
BORDER FEATURE FILM CORPORATION, *Bisbee and Tombstone, Ariz.*
BRADLEY FEATURE FILM COMPANY, 2147 *Prospect Ave., Cleveland, Ohio.*
BRENTWOOD FILM CORPORATION, 4811 *Fountain Ave., Hollywood, Cal.*
BREWSTER-KEMBLE PRODUCTIONS, 7100 *Santa Monica Blvd., Hollywood, Cal.*
ROBERT BRUNTON PRODUCTIONS, 5341-5601 *Melrose Ave., Los Angeles, Cal.*
BRUNTON STUDIOS, 5341-5601 *Melrose Ave., Los Angeles, Cal.*
BURSTON FILMS, 6050 *Sunset Blvd., Hollywood, Cal.*
DAVID BUTLER PRODUCTIONS, 5341-5601 *Melrose Ave., Hollywood, Cal.*
WILLIAM CHRISTY CABANNE PRODUCTIONS, 780 *Gower Street, Hollywood, Cal.*
CALIFORNIA PRODUCERS CORPORATION, 7100 *Santa Monica Blvd., Hollywood, Cal.*
ANDREW J. CALLAHAN PRODUCTIONS, 5542 *Santa Monica Blvd., Hollywood, Cal.*
CAMPBELL COMEDY COMPANY, 4534 *Sunset Blvd., Hollywood, Cal.*
LLOYD CARLETON PRODUCTIONS, 6070 *Sunset Blvd., Hollywood, Cal.*
CELEBRATED PLAYERS FILM CORPORATION, 810 *S. Wabash Ave., Chicago, Ill.*
CENTURY FILM CORPORATION, 6100 *Sunset Blvd., Hollywood, Cal.*
CHARLES CHAPLIN FILM CORPORATION, 1420 *La Brea Ave., Hollywood, Cal.*
C. L. CHESTER PRODUCTIONS, 1438 *Gower Street, Hollywood, Cal.*
CHRISTIE FILM COMPANY, 6101 *Sunset Blvd., Hollywood, Cal.*
CINAL FILMS, 7870 *Santa Monica Blvd., Hollywood, Cal.*
CINART, INC., 614 *Hollingsworth Bldg., Los Angeles, Cal.*
CINEMACRAFT, INC., 735 *Van Nuys Bldg., Los Angeles, Cal.*
CLEVER COMEDIES, 6040 *Sunset Blvd., Hollywood, Cal.*
CLOVERIO FILM COMPANY, *Lents, Portland, Ore.*
CLUNE STUDIO AND LABORATORIES, 5320 *Melrose Ave., Los Angeles, Cal.*
COMMONWEALTH PICTURE CORPORATION, 220 *South State Street, Chicago, Ill.*
CORTLAND PICTURES CORP., *Hume-Mansur Bldg., Indianapolis, Ind.*
COSMOPOLITAN PRODUCTIONS, 2478 *Second Avenue, N. Y.*
CREATION FILMS, INC., 220 *South State Street, Chicago, Ill.*
CARTER DE HAVEN PRODUCTIONS, 3800 *Mission Road, Hollywood, Cal.*
WILLIAM DESMOND PRODUCTIONS, 5341 *Melrose Ave., Los Angeles, Cal.*
DIAL FILM COMPANY, 5341 *Melrose Ave., Los Angeles, Cal.*
DIERKER FILM COMPANY, 1023 *Van Nuys Bldg., Los Angeles, Cal.*
DOUBLEDAY PRODUCTION COMPANY, 426 *Byrne Bldg., Los Angeles, Cal.*
DOUGLAS NATURAL COLOR FILM CO., LTD., *San Rafael, Cal.*
DRASCENA PRODUCTIONS, *Haas Bldg., Los Angeles, Cal.*
ALLAN DWAN PRODUCTIONS, 6642 *Santa Monica Blvd., Hollywood, Cal.*
DOUGLAS FAIRBANKS PICTURES CORPORATION, 5320 *Melrose Ave., Hollywood, Cal.*
MARION FAIRFAX PRODUCTIONS, 6642 *Santa Monica Blvd., Hollywood, Cal.*
FAMOUS PLAYERS WEST COAST STUDIOS, 1520 *Vine Street, Hollywood, Cal.*
ROBERT L. FARGO PRODUCTIONS, 1116 *Lodi Street, Hollywood, Cal.*

FEDERAL PHOTOPLAYS OF CALIFORNIA, 5341 *Melrose Ave., Los Angeles, Cal.*
FILMCRAFT LABORATORY, *Culver City, Cal.*
FRANCIS FORD STUDIOS, 6040 *Sunset Blvd., Hollywood, Cal.*
● FOX STUDIOS, 1417 *N. Western Ave., Hollywood, Cal.*
J. L. FROTHINGHAM PRODUCTIONS, 5341 *Melrose Ave., Hollywood, Cal.*
GARSON STUDIOS, INC., 1845 *Glendale Blvd., Los Angeles, Cal.*
PAUL GERSON PICTURES CORPORATION, 353-361 *Tenth Street, San Francisco, Cal.*
● GOLDWYN STUDIOS, *Culver City, Cal.*
ARTHUR H. GOODEN STUDIOS, 4534 *Sunset Blvd., Hollywood, Cal.*
GREAT AUTHORS PICTURES CORPORATION, 5341 *Melrose Ave., Los Angeles, Cal.*
GREAT WESTERN PRODUCING COMPANY, 6100 *Sunset Blvd., Hollywood, Cal.*
GRIEVER DISTRIBUTING CORPORATION, 207 *S. Wabash Ave., Chicago, Ill.*
● D. W. GRIFFITH STUDIOS, *Mamaroneck, L. I., N. Y.*
ZANE GREY PICTURES CORPORATION, 5341 *Melrose Ave., Los Angeles, Cal.*
● HAMILTON-WHITE COMEDIES, 4534 *Sunset Blvd., Hollywood, Cal.*
● BENJAMIN B. HAMPTON PRODUCTIONS, 5341 *Melrose Ave., Los Angeles, Cal.*
JESSE HAMPTON PRODUCTIONS, 7100 *Santa Monica Blvd., Hollywood, Cal.*
HARMONY FILM COMPANY, 405 *Courier Bldg., Los Angeles, Cal.*
● HART PRODUCTIONS, 7100 *Santa Monica Blvd., Hollywood, Cal.*
● WILLIAM S. HART PRODUCTIONS, *Apollo Theatre Bldg., Hollywood, Cal.*
DAVID M. HARTFORD PRODUCTIONS, 3274 *West Sixth Street, Los Angeles, Cal.*
HARTER-WALL PRODUCTIONS, *Bakersfield, Cal.*
HERMANN FILM CORPORATION, 2435 *Wilshire Blvd., San Monica, Cal.*
HOLLYWOOD STUDIOS, 6642 *Santa Monica Blvd., Hollywood, Cal.*
BURTON HOLMES LABORATORY, 7510 *N. Ashland Ave., Chicago, Ill.*
● WILLIAM HORSLEY FILM LABORATORIES, 6060 *Sunset Blvd., Hollywood, Cal.*
ARTHUR S. HYMAN PRODUCTIONS, *Consumers Bldg., Chicago, Ill.*
THOMAS H. INCE STUDIOS, *Culver City, Cal.*
INTERNATIONAL PHOTOPLAY CORPORATION, 3501 *N. Kenton Ave., Chicago, Ill.*
INTERNATIONAL FILM SERVICE, 2478 *Second Ave., N. Y.*
JACQUELIN FILM COMPANY, *Reelcraft Studios, Chicago, Ill.*
JUVENILE PHOTOPLAY COMPANY, 310 *Sloan Bldg., Cleveland, Ohio.*
K. & K PRODUCTIONS, 6070 *Sunset Blvd., Hollywood, Cal.*
KIPLING FILM EXCHANGE, INC., 802 *S. Olive Street, Los Angeles, Cal.*
RICHARD KIPLING ENTERPRISES, 802 *S. Olive Street, Los Angeles, Cal.*
● GEORGE KLEINE, 63 *E. Adams Street, Chicago, Ill.*
VICTOR KREMER FILM FEATURES, *Francis Ford Studios,* 6040 *Sunset Blvd., Hollywood, Cal.*
● L-KO PICTURE COMPANY, *Universal Studios, Universal City, Cal.*
LOCAL PRODUCTIONS, 224 *O. T. Johnson Bldg., Los Angeles, Cal.*
LA SALLE FILM COMPANY, 1450 *Dayton Street, Chicago, Ill.*
SOL LESSER ENTERPRISES, 643 *S. Olive Street, Los Angeles, Cal.*
EDGAR LEWIS PRODUCTIONS, 1119 *Westchester Place, Hollywood, Cal.*
LINCOLN MOTION PICTURE COMPANY, 1121 *Central Ave., Los Angeles, Cal.*
● MAX LINDER PRODUCTIONS, *Universal City, Cal.*
● HAROLD LLOYD COMEDIES, *Roach Studios, Culver City, Cal.*
● LONE STAR FILM PRODUCTIONS, 1745 *Glendale Blvd., Hollywood, Cal.*
● HANK MANN COMPANY, 1439 *Beechwood Drive, Hollywood, Cal.*
LOUIS B. MAYER PRODUCTIONS, 3800 *Mission Road, Hollywood, Cal.*
MAYFLOWER PICTURES CORPORATION, 5341 *Melrose Ave., Los Angeles, Cal.*
McCARTHY PICTURE CORPORATION, 500 *Markham Bldg., Hollywood, Cal.*
JACK MacCULLOUGH COMPANY, 1825 *Warren Ave., Chicago, Ill.*
MENA FILM COMPANY, *Foundation and Berando Streets, Hollywood, Cal.*
● MERMAID' COMEDIES, *Astra Studios, Verdugo Road, Glendale, Cal.*
METRO STUDIOS, 900 *Cahuenga Street, Hollywood, Cal.*
MICHEAUX FILM CORP., 538 *S. Dearborn Street, Chicago, Ill.*
A. LINCOLN MILLER PRODUCTIONS, 1139 *Coronado Terrace, Los Angeles, Cal.*
MOLINA FILM CORPORATION, *Anaheim, Cal.*
● OLIVER MOROSCO PRODUCTIONS, 756 *S. Broadway, Los Angeles, Cal.*
NATIONAL FILM CORP. OF AMERICA, 1116 *Lodi Street, Hollywood, Cal.*
● MARSHALL NEILAN PRODUCTIONS, 6642 *Santa Monica Blvd., Hollywood, Cal.*
NOVAGRAPH FILM COMPANY, 923 *Cole Ave., Los Angeles, Cal.*
PACIFIC FILM COMPANY, 780 *S. Olive Street, Los Angeles, Cal.*
PACIFIC STUDIOS CORPORATION, *San Mateo, Cal.*
PALMER PHOTOPLAY CORP., *I. W. Hellman Bldg., Los Angeles, Cal.*
● PATHE STUDIOS, 1990 *Park Ave., N. Y.*
PATRICIAN PRODUCTIONS, INC., 1400 *Merchants Bank Bldg., San Francisco, Cal.*

MARY PICKFORD FILM COMPANY, 5341 *Melrose Ave., Los Angeles, Cal.*
PINNACLE PRODUCTIONS, 6575 *Fountain Ave., Hollywood, Cal.*
SNUB POLLARD COMEDIES, *Roach Studios, Culver City, Cal.*
DOLLY PRITCHARD PICTURES, *International Bldg., Los Angeles, Cal.*
PRODUCERS FILM COMPANY, *Oroville, Cal.*
PRODUCERS PICTURES CORP., 6642 *Santa Monica Blvd., Hollywood, Cal.*
PYGMY PICTURES, INC., *Western Mutual Life Bldg., Los Angeles, Cal.*
QUALITY PICTURES CORPORATION, 526 *Holbrook Bldg., San Francisco, Cal.*
R-C PICTURES CORPORATION, *Studio, Hollywood, Cal.*
R-D FILM CORPORATION, *Long Beach, Cal.*
CHARLES RAY PRODUCTIONS, 1425 *Fleming Street, Los Angeles, Cal.*
J. PARKER READ, JR., PRODUCTIONS, *Ince Studio, Culver City, Cal.*
REALART STUDIOS, 201-211 N. *Occidental Blvd., Los Angeles, Cal.*
REELCRAFT PICTURES CORPORATION, 1107 *Bronson Ave., Hollywood, Cal.*
RENCO FILM COMPANY, 724 S. *Spring Street, Los Angeles, Cal.*
HAL E. ROACH STUDIO, INC., *Culver City, Cal.*
ROBERTSON-COLE STUDIOS, 780 *Gower Street, Hollywood, Cal.*
ROCKETT FILM CORPORATION, *Hollywood, Cal., Studio,* 3800 *Mission Road, Hollywood, Cal.*
RUTH ROLAND PRODUCTIONS, *Culver City, Cal.*
ROLIN FILM COMPANY, *Roach Studios, Culver City, Cal.*
ROMAYNE SUPERFILM COMPANY, *Culver City, Cal.*
RUSSELL PRODUCTION STUDIO, 6070 *Sunset Blvd., Hollywood, Cal.*
SACRED FILMS, INC., *Burbank, Cal.*
MORRIS R. SCHLANK PRODUCTIONS, 1439 *Beechwood Drive, Hollywood, Cal.*
EDNA SCHLEY PRODUCTIONS, 6372 *Hollywood Blvd., Hollywood, Cal.*
SELIG-RORK, 3800 *Mission Road, Los Angeles, Cal.*
SELZNICK STUDIOS, *West Fort Lee, N. J.*
LARRY SEMON COMEDIES, *Vitagraph Studios,* 1708 *Talmadge Street, Hollywood, Cal.*
MACK SENNETT COMEDIES, INC., 1712 *Glendale Blvd., Los Angeles, Cal.*
NELL SHIPMAN PRODUCTIONS, 643 S. *Olive Street, Los Angeles, Cal.*
SIGNAL FILM CORPORATION, 6227-6235 *Broadway, Chicago, Ill.*
CLIFF SMITH PRODUCTIONS, 1511 *Cahuenga Ave., Hollywood, Cal.*
SPENCER PRODUCTIONS, 2435 *Wilshire Blvd., Santa Monica, Cal.*
JOHN M. STAHL PRODUCTIONS, 3800 *Mission Road, Hollywood, Cal.*
STANDARD FILM LABORATORIES, 130 *West Fifth Street, Los Angeles, Cal.*
TATTENHAM PRODUCTIONS, 4534 *Sunset Blvd., Hollywood, Cal.*
MAURICE TOURNEUR PRODUCTIONS, *Ince Studios, Culver City, Cal.*
UNION FILM COMPANY, *Sherman, Cal.*
UNIVERSAL FILM MANUFACTURING CO., *Universal City, Cal.*
KING VIDOR PRODUCTIONS, 7100 *Santa Monica Blvd., Hollywood, Cal.*
VITAGRAPH STUDIOS, 1708 *Talmadge Street, Hollywood, Cal.*
VITAGRAPH STUDIOS, *Brooklyn, N. Y.*
WAH MING MOTION PICTURE COMPANY, 758 S. *Boyle Street, Los Angeles, Cal.*
R. A. WALSH PRODUCTIONS, 5341 *Melrose Ave., Los Angeles, Cal.*
WARNER BROTHERS' STUDIO, *Bronson Ave. and Sunset Blvd., Hollywood, Cal.*
LOIS WEBER PRODUCTIONS, 4634 *Santa Monica Blvd., Los Angeles, Cal.*
BILLY WEST COMEDIES, 1116 *Lodi Street, Hollywood, Cal.*
WESTERN FEATURE PRODUCTIONS, 5545 *Hollywood Blvd., Hollywood, Cal.*
WESTERN PICTURES EXPLOITATION COMPANY, H. W. *Hellman Bldg., Los Angeles, Cal.*
WESTERN STAR PRODUCTIONS, 620 *Sunset Blvd., Hollywood, Cal.*
WILLAT PRODUCTIONS, *Culver City, Cal.*
CYRUS J. WILLIAMS PRODUCTIONS, 4811 *Fountain Ave., Hollywood, Cal.*
BEN WILSON PRODUCTIONS, 5821 *Santa Monica Blvd., Hollywood, Cal.*
WONDERGRAF PRODUCTIONS CORPORATION, 6050 *Sunset Blvd., Hollywood, Cal.*
HAROLD BELL WRIGHT STORY PICTURES CORP., 1511 *Cahuenga Street, Los Angeles, Cal.*
CLARA KIMBALL YOUNG PRODUCTIONS, *Garson Studios,* 1845 *Glendale Blvd., Los Angeles, Cal.*
ZENITH FEATURES, INC., *Mayer Studios,* 3800 *Mission Road, Hollywood, Cal.*
LIVINGSTON PRODUCTIONS, 2435 *Wilshire Blvd., Santa Monica, Cal.*
ITALIAN-AMERICAN FILM CORPORATION, 403 *Douglas Bldg., Los Angeles, Cal.*
REGGIE MORRIS PRODUCTIONS, 5828 *Santa Monica Blvd., Hollywood, Cal.*